To Woo
& To Wed

CONTEMPORARY
POETS ON LOVE
& MARRIAGE

EDITED BY
Michael Blumenthal

POSEIDON PRESS
New York   London   Toronto
Sydney   Tokyo   Singapore

POSEIDON PRESS

Simon & Schuster Building
Rockefeller Center
1230 Avenue of the Americas
New York, New York 10020

DESIGNED BY BARBARA MARKS
Manufactured in the United States of America

10 9 8 7 6 5 4 3 2 1
10 9 8 7 6 5 4 3 2 1

Library of Congress Cataloging-in-Publication Data

To woo & to wed : contemporary poets on love &
marriage / edited by Michael Blumenthal.
p. cm.
Originally published (© 1992) without
"contemporary" in the subtitle.
1. Love—Poetry. 2. Marriage—Poetry.
I. Blumenthal, Michael.
II. Title: To woo and to wed.
PN6110.L6T6 1993
808.81'9354—dc20   92-25173
CIP

ISBN: 0-671-72347-2
ISBN: 0-671-79645-3 (pbk)

First Poseidon Press Trade Paperback Printing 1993

Permission to reprint copyrighted poems is
gratefully acknowledged in the
Acknowledgments section on page 255.

For Isabelle & Noah

and for Ross, Marilyn & Adrian
in whose friendship all are married

Contents

VII A MAN AND A WOMAN

VIII THE ACHE OF MARRIAGE

IX FROM GRIEF TO GRIEF

X LOVE RECOGNIZED

Introduction

"POETRY," the Danish philosopher Søren Kierkegaard remarked in a long essay entitled "Reflections on Marriage," "cannot use a married man." What Kierkegaard meant, quite explicitly, was that the poet (or, at least, a highly romantic notion of the poet) "is great by virtue of his faith in immediacy and in its power to force its way through," whereas married men and women, as Robert Graves so tellingly puts it in his poem, "The Wedding," "howl for their lost immediacy."

But poetry, of course, always *has* used married men, and married women—from Milton to Yeats, from Sappho to Edna St. Vincent Millay, from Shakespeare to Anne Sexton. Indeed, marriage has, throughout history and across cultures, been one of poetry's great subjects, one of its seemingly timeless metaphors. So much, in fact, has been said, and written, about marriage—in poetry, fiction, philosophy, religion, and journalism—that it clearly qualifies as one of humankind's central concerns, the triumph, perhaps, of our entire species' hope over experience.

"Any marriage," the poet W. H. Auden once remarked, "happy or unhappy, is infinitely more interesting and significant than any romance, however passionate." The truth of Auden's observation—and I believe it to be true—may derive from the fact that, whereas romance offers only an endless repetition of the same simultaneously exhilarating and painful emotional arc, each marriage—and not *just* unhappy ones, as Tolstoy would have us believe of families in general—is somehow unique, complex, and endlessly mysterious. For romance, as Joseph Epstein has pointed out, must leave off at the point of "happily ever after"; whereas marriage concerns itself with that decisive "after."

Indeed, whether it is true, as Oscar Wilde suggests, that men marry because they are tired and women because they are curious (and that both are disappointed), or that we all marry, according to Plato, because we are in search of the perfectly integrated souls we were in a previous life, or because, in Kierkegaard's words, marriage is "the most beautiful form of human happiness," one thing is certain: most of us, for better *and* worse, *do* marry. Something—whether it is a sociobiological survival act, a deep psychological need for security, or something so complex and mysterious that we can do no better than group it loosely under the ever-mysterious orbit of the word *love*—drives most of us to marry and (perhaps even more astonishingly) when marriage fails, to marry again.

For marriage, as Emerson observed, seems to be the perfection love aims at, though it may also (as he immediately added) be ignorant of what it has sought . . . or may fail to achieve it. "My main theme," Robert Graves wrote in the preface to his *Collected Poems,* "was always the practical impossibility, transcended only by a belief in miracle, of absolute love continuing between man and woman." Yet so tenacious do we (Graves included!) seem to be in constantly enacting and reenacting our hopes to become part of that "happy nuptial league" Milton speaks of in *Paradise Lost* that it might be said of our collective attitude toward marriage that it more closely resembles Winston Churchill's sentiments about democracy: namely, that it is the worst possible system—until we compare it with all the other possibilities.

But marriage, it also seems to me, is also more than merely, as has been suggested, the triumph of the dread of loneliness over the fear of bondage. It is also a triumph of another kind: the triumph of our need for connection, comfort, family, reliability, nurturance, and partnership over our need for ego-centered conquest, solitude, and separateness, though separate we certainly are. For though the "bride bed," as Yeats suggests, *may* well "bring despair," it is no doubt also true that a certain world (the world of our separateness, our loneliness, our isolation, our essential sense of our own meaninglessness) *may* come to an end when "these two things"—husband and wife, man and man, woman and woman, yin and yang—"form a single light."

Indeed, my own favorite definition of marriage—the Rilkean ideal of a partnership in which each is appointed guardian of the other's solitude—seems more like an inspired synthesis of those two extremes, an attempt to navigate between the Scylla of loneliness and isolation and the Charybdis of bondage.

Some years ago, a very bright student of mine came into my office and began conversing with me about her theory that tragedies like Shakespeare's *Othello* couldn't possibly be written in our time. "Why?" I asked, curious as to how my precociously wise undergraduate friend would respond. "Because, today, Othello's jealousy wouldn't have had the time to fester and expand the way it does in the play . . . He and Desdemona would be too busy 'sharing' their feelings or talking it over with a therapist for the emotions to do their dirty work 'underground.' "

Indeed, the kind of demystification my student was talking about *has* taken place in the poetry of marriage as well, so that the kind of "impediments" Shakespeare speaks of in his famous sonnet now exist, outspokenly, even in the expressions of "true minds." Yet marriage, even in this post-Freudian era of our self-scrutiny and dark knowing, remains a kind of Kierkegaardian "leap of faith," a constantly reenacted "belief in miracle" of the kind Robert Graves was perhaps suggesting.

Given the realities, then, of modern life and psyche—and notwithstanding the sentimental occasion marriage has always been and will, gratefully, always continue to be (for we deeply need so-called "sentimental" occasions as well as harshly realistic ones)—no contemporary anthology of marriage poems can afford not to reflect our increasing consciousness of marriage's obvious darknesses and dangers. So that, in this volume for example, we have even as affirmingly married and committed a poet as Wendell Berry acknowledging, in "The Country of Marriage," that "The forest is mostly dark, its ways/ to be made anew day after day, the dark/ richer than the light and more blessed,/ provided we stay brave/ enough to keep on going in."

And we *do* "keep on going in"—full of hope and fear and consciousness and unconsciousness, full of mystifications and demystifications and triumphs and regrets. For marriage, if it is nothing else, is certainly a microcosm of our lives—our yearning for attachment and our difficulties with it; our effort at self-transcendence and our perpetual failure (and reattempt) at it. Whether we ask—in the spirit of Virginia Woolf—for someone to "make (us) vehement" or—in the spirit of Matthew Arnold—for someone to offer us comfort in a world that "Hath really neither joy, nor love, nor light/ Nor certitude, nor peace, nor help for pain," it is clear that what we are asking for in a marriage partner, in the end, is a kind of completion, a hope for a better and more endurable harmony in a world where harmony—either in or *out* of marriage—is not easily achieved.

What I have tried to assemble here—in the form, mostly, of contemporary English-language (or recently translated) poets who have added their collective wisdom and experience to what Robert Louis Stevenson described as the "one long conversation checkered by disputes" that is marriage—is an anthology that would reflect the realities of marriage in all its hopefulness, ambivalence, celebration, disappointment, anger, sadness, and mystery . . . in other words, in all its profound and beautiful complexity. If, in the end, marriage—as Emily Dickinson said of parting—may well contain "all we know of heaven/ and all we need to know of hell," it may yet be, as Kierkegaard said, "the most important voyage of discovery a human being undertakes."

Like any anthologist, I have no doubt failed, at least in part. No doubt, some poets have been included who should, in some readers' eyes, have been omitted, and some omitted who should have been included. For every anthology is, in the end, also a compilation of compromises and prejudices, oversights and omissions. And even an anthologist must, at some point, *stop* reading! The fact that in several cases (i.e., Wendell Berry, Linda Pastan, Ellen Bryant Voigt, Alan Feldman, Stephen Dunn, and others) I have included a small handful of poems by the same poet simply reflects my own sense that there are certain contemporary poets for whom marriage is a true "subject," rather than merely an occasion, a matter of ultimate concern rather than a touristic visit to largely unfamiliar terrain.

There is also here, as in any "subject-oriented" anthology, the obvious tension between the making of an anthology of *poetry* and the creation of an anthology centered around a *subject* . . . the frequent dilemma of choosing at times, perhaps, a slightly "lesser" poem from a purely aesthetic point of view, but one that may more accurately (and more poignantly) hit the emotional mark. As in marriage itself perhaps, the realities of having to find a workable compromise between purely aesthetic considerations and more practical ones may lead to the worst of both worlds . . . or, one hopes, to the best possible synthesis of the two. When in doubt, I have tended to choose those poems that would be more available to a general, not necessarily "literary" audience over those whose difficulties would be more of a joy to other poets than to a general, albeit interested, reader. This, perhaps, reflects my own prejudice slightly away from T. S. Eliot's "joy of the difficult" to the more available joys of poems that are both accessible *and* moving.

Lastly, I must confess that I have been working on this book for the past year with the voice of at least one other poet constantly whispering a certain dark and ominous message in my ear . . . a message that any poet working as an anthologist ought, perhaps, to be mindful of. The voice is that of the late Nobel Prize–winning Italian poet, Eugenio Montale, who—in a bitingly satirical essay entitled "The Poet" written in 1951—wrote:

The poet isn't fond of other poets, but from time to time he turns into an anthologist and collector of the poems of others so that he can include his own as well. He's obeying a "scruple of objectivity," a scientific duty. It's not that it matters to him, but posterity must be informed.

Having, for the moment at least, become an anthologist, and having not hesitated to include a certain none-too-small handful of my own poems, I think it would be an act of false innocence not also to subject myself to the scrutiny of Montale's words.

With that in mind, I have tried to include poems of my own in good faith, and with a sense that it might be no accident that a poet motivated to compile such an anthology would also have been motivated in his own work to concern himself with its subject. If I have exercised bad (or good) taste in choosing my own work, I can only hope that it is the same good or bad taste I have exercised in choosing anyone else's. . . . If not, I can only say that I don't deserve to be spared the implicit condemnation of Montale's words.

Lastly, I want to extend my thanks to several people who were kind and generous enough to offer me advice and encouragement in compiling this volume. First of all, to my agent, Flip Brophy, and my publisher, Ann Patty, for their faith in this project, and to Fonda Duvanel of Poseidon Press. Then to my good-natured, reliable, wisely discriminating research assistant, Elizabeth Esty, with the sincere hope that having had to read so many poems about marriage will not have frightened her away from the enterprise therein described. Then to Tony Deninger, Melanie Thernstrom, Seamus Heaney, Helen Vendler, Grace Schulman, and Susan Kinsolving, who so generously offered suggestions and ideas for inclusion.

Most of all, however, I am grateful to my wife Isabelle—not so much for the usual authorial platitudes about patience and forbearance, but for teaching me enough about what marriage really *is* so that making a book of this sort felt not like an act of hypocrisy, but like an act of love.

Cambridge, Massachusetts
JULY 1991

I

Because

Love's Philosophy

The Fountains mingle with the River
    And the Rivers with the Ocean,
The winds of Heaven mix for ever
    With a sweet emotion;
Nothing in the world is single;
    All things by a law divine
In one spirit meet and mingle.
    Why not I with thine?—

See the mountains kiss high Heaven
    And the waves clasp one another;
No sister-flower would be forgiven
    If it disdained its brother,
And the sunlight clasps the earth
    And the moonbeams kiss the sea:
What is all this sweet work worth
    If thou kiss not me?

PERCY BYSSHE SHELLEY

Will you perhaps consent to be
("méntre il vento, come fa, si tace")

Will you perhaps consent to be
Now that a little while is still
(Ruth of sweet wind) now that a little while
My mind's continuing and unreleasing wind
Touches this single of your flowers, this one only,
Will you perhaps consent to be
My many-branched, small and dearest tree?

My mind's continuing and unreleasing wind
—The wind which is wild and restless, tired and asleep,
The wind which is tired, wild and still continuing,
The wind which is chill, and warm, wet, soft, in every
    influence,
Lusts for Paris, Crete and Pergamus,
Is suddenly off for Paris and Chicago,
Judaea, San Francisco, the Midi
—May I perhaps return to you
Wet with an Arctic dust and chill from Norway
My dear, so-many-branched smallest tree?

Would you perhaps consent to be
The very rack and crucifix of winter, winter's wild
Knife-edged, continuing and unreleasing,
Intent and stripping, ice-caressing wind?
My dear, most dear, so-many-branched tree,
My mind's continuing and unreleasing wind
Touches this single of your flowers, faith in me,
Wide as the—sky!—accepting as the (air)!
—Consent, consent, consent to be
My many-branched, small and dearest tree.

DELMORE SCHWARTZ

from *Notes toward a Supreme Fiction*

Two things of opposite natures seem to depend
On one another, as a man depends
On a woman, day on night, the imagined

On the real. This is the origin of change.
Winter and spring, cold copulars, embrace
And forth the particulars of rapture come.

Music falls on the silence like a sense,
A passion that we feel, not understand.
Morning and afternoon are clasped together

And North and South are an intrinsic couple
And sun and rain a plural, like two lovers
That walk away as one in the greenest body.

In solitude the trumpets of solitude
Are not of another solitude resounding;
A little string speaks for a crowd of voices.

The partaker partakes of that which changes him.
The child that touches takes character from the thing,
The body, it touches. The captain and his men

Are one and the sailor and the sea are one.
Follow after, O my companion, my fellow, my self,
Sister and solace, brother and delight.

WALLACE STEVENS

Marriage

Romance is a world, tiny and curved, reflected in a spoon. Perilous as a clean sheet of paper. Why begin? Why sully and crumple a perfectly good surface? Lots of reasons. Sensuality, need for relief, curiosity. Or it's your mission. You could blame the mating instinct: a squat little god carved from shit-colored wood. NO NO NO. It's not dirty. The plight of desire, a longing to consort, to dally, bend over, lose yourself; be rubbed till you're shiny as a new minted utensil. A monogrammed butter knife, modern pattern or heirloom. It's a time of plagues and lapses, rips in the ozone layer's bridal veil. One must take comfort in whatever lap one can. He wanted her to bite him, lightly. She wanted to drink a quart of water and get to bed early. Now that's what I call an exciting date. In the voodoo religion, believers can marry their gods. Some nuns wed Jesus, but they have to cut off all their hair first. He's afraid he'll tangle in it, trip and fall. Be laid low. Get lost. Your face, lovely and rough as a gravestone. I kiss it. I do.

In a more pragmatic age many brides' veils later served as their burying shrouds. After they'd paid their dues to mother nature, they commanded last respects. Wreaths, incense and satin in crypts. In India marriage of children is common. An army of those who died young march through your studio this afternoon to rebuke you for closing your eyes to the fullness of the world. But when they get close enough to read what's written on your forehead, they realize you only did what was necessary. Then they hurriedly skip outside to bless your car, your mangy lawn and the silver floss tree which bows down in your front yard.

His waiting room is full of pious heathens and the pastor calls them into his office for counseling, two by two. Once you caressed me in a restaurant by poking me with a fork. In those days, any embrace was a strain. In the picture in this encyclopedia, the oriental bride's headdress looks like a paper boat. The caption says "Marriage in Japan is a formal, solemn ceremony." O bride fed and bedded down on a sea of dexatrim, tea, rice and quinine, can you guide me? Is the current swift? Is there a bridge? What does this old fraction add up to: you over me? Mr. Numerator on top of Miss Denominator? The two of us divided by a line from a psalm, a differing line of thinking, the thin bloodless line of your lips pressed together. At the end of the service guests often toss rice or old shoes. You had a close shave, handsome. Almost knocked unconscious by a flying army boot, while your friends continued to converse nonchalantly under the canopy of mosquito netting. You never recognized me, darling, but I knew you right away. I know my fate when I see it. But it's bad luck to lay eyes on each other before the appropriate moment. So look away. Even from this distance, and the chasm is widening, the room grows huge, I kiss your old and new wounds. I kiss you. I do.

AMY GERSTLER

Marriage

Should I get married? Should I be good?
Astound the girl next door with my velvet suit and faustus hood?
Don't take her to movies but to cemeteries
tell all about werewolf bathtubs and forked clarinets
then desire her and kiss her and all the preliminaries
and she going just so far and I understanding why
not getting angry saying You must feel! It's beautiful to feel!
Instead take her in my arms lean against an old crooked tombstone
and woo her the entire night the constellations in the sky—

When she introduces me to her parents
back straightened, hair finally combed, strangled by a tie,
should I sit knees together on their 3rd degree sofa
and not ask Where's the bathroom?
How else to feel other than I am,
often thinking Flash Gordon soap—
O how terrible it must be for a young man
seated before a family and the family thinking
We never saw him before! He wants our Mary Lou!
After tea and homemade cookies they ask What do you do for a living?
Should I tell them? Would they like me then?
Say All right get married, we're losing a daughter
but we're gaining a son—
And should I then ask Where's the bathroom?

O God, and the wedding! All her family and her friends
and only a handful of mine all scroungy and bearded
just wait to get at the drinks and food—
And the priest! he looking at me as if I masturbated
asking me Do you take this woman for your lawful wedded wife?
And I trembling what to say say Pie Glue!
I kiss the bride all those corny men slapping me on the back
She's all yours, boy! Ha-ha-ha!
And in their eyes you could see some obscene honeymoon going on—
Then all that absurd rice and clanky cans and shoes
Niagara Falls! Hordes of us! Husbands! Wives! Flowers! Chocolates!
All streaming into cozy hotels
All going to do the same thing tonight
The indifferent clerk he knowing what was going to happen
The lobby zombies they knowing what
The whistling elevator man he knowing

The winking bellboy knowing
Everybody knowing! I'd be almost inclined not to do anything!
Stay up all night! Stare that hotel clerk in the eye!
Screaming: I deny honeymoon! I deny honeymoon!
running rampant into those almost climactic suites
yelling Radio belly! Cat shovel!
O I'd live in Niagara forever! in a dark cave beneath the Falls
I'd sit there the Mad Honeymooner
devising ways to break marriages, a scourge of bigamy
a saint of divorce—

But I should get married I should be good
How nice it'd be to come home to her
and sit by the fireplace and she in the kitchen
aproned young and lovely wanting my baby
and so happy about me she burns the roast beef
and comes crying to me and I get up from my big papa chair
saying Christmas teeth! Radiant brains! Apple deaf!
God what a husband I'd make! Yes, I should get married!
So much to do! like sneaking into Mr Jones' house late at night
and cover his golf clubs with 1920 Norwegian books
Like hanging a picture of Rimbaud on the lawnmower
like pasting Tannu Tuva postage stamps all over the picket fence
like when Mrs Kindhead comes to collect for the Community Chest
grab her and tell her There are unfavorable omens in the sky!
And when the mayor comes to get my vote tell him
When are you going to stop people killing whales!
And when the milkman comes leave him a note in the bottle
Penguin dust, bring me penguin dust, I want penguin dust—

Yet if I should get married and it's Connecticut and snow
and she gives birth to a child and I am sleepless, worn,
up for nights, head bowed against a quiet window, the past behind me,
finding myself in the most common of situations a trembling man
knowledged with responsibility not twig-smear nor Roman coin
        soup—
O what would that be like!
Surely I'd give it for a nipple a rubber Tacitus
For a rattle a bag of broken Bach records
Tack Della Francesca all over its crib
Sew the Greek alphabet on its bib
And build for its playpen a roofless Parthenon

(break)

No, I doubt I'd be that kind of father
not rural not snow no quiet window
but hot smelly tight New York City
seven flights up roaches and rats in the walls
a fat Reichian wife screeching over potatoes Get a job!
And five nose running brats in love with Batman
And the neighbors all toothless and dry haired
like those hag masses of the 18th century
all wanting to come in and watch TV
The landlord wants his rent
Grocery store Blue Cross Gas & Electric Knights of Columbus
Impossible to lie back and dream Telephone snow, ghost parking—
No! I should not get married I should never get married!
But—imagine If I were married to a beautiful sophisticated woman
tall and pale wearing an elegant black dress and long black gloves
holding a cigarette holder in one hand and a highball in the other
and we lived high up in a penthouse with a huge window
from which we could see all of New York and ever farther on clearer
        days
No, can't imagine myself married to that pleasant prison dream—

O but what about love? I forget love
not that I am incapable of love
it's just that I see love as odd as wearing shoes—
I never wanted to marry a girl who was like my mother
And Ingrid Bergman was always impossible
And there's maybe a girl now but she's already married
And I don't like men and—
but there's got to be somebody!
Because what if I'm 60 years old and not married,
all alone in a furnished room with pee stains on my underwear
and everybody else is married! All the universe married but me!

Ah, yet well I know that were a woman possible as I am possible
then marriage would be possible—
Like SHE in her lonely alien gaud waiting her Egyptian lover
so I wait—bereft of 2,000 years and the bath of life.

GREGORY CORSO

Advice for Good Love

Advice for good love: Don't love
those from far away. Take yourself one
from nearby.
The way a sensible house will take
local stones for its building,
stones which have suffered in the same cold
and were scorched by the same sun.
Take the one with the golden wreath
around her dark eye's pupil, she
who has a certain knowledge
about your death. Love also inside
ruins like taking honey out of
the lion's carcass that Samson killed.

And advice for bad love: With
the love left over
from the previous one
make a new woman for yourself,
then with what is left of that woman
make again a new love,
and go on like that
until nothing remains for you.

YEHUDA AMICHAI

Men Marry What They Need

Men marry what they need. I marry you,
morning by morning, day by day, night by night,
and every marriage makes this marriage new.

In the broken name of heaven, in the light
that shatters granite, by the spitting shore,
in air that leaps and wobbles like a kite,

I marry you from time and a great door
is shut and stays shut against wind, sea, stone,
sunburst, and heavenfall. And home once more

inside our walls of skin and struts of bone,
man-woman, woman-man, and each the other,
I marry you by all dark and all dawn

and have my laugh at death. Why should I bother
the flies about me? Let them buzz and do.
Men marry their queen, their daughter, or their mother

by hidden names, but that thin buzz whines through:
where reasons are no reason, cause is true.
Men marry what they need. I marry you.

JOHN CIARDI

A Slice of Wedding Cake

Why have such scores of lovely, gifted girls
    Married impossible men?
Simple self-sacrifice may be ruled out,
    And missionary endeavour, nine times out of ten.

Repeat 'impossible men': not merely rustic,
    Foul-tempered or depraved
(Dramatic foils chosen to show the world
    How well women behave, and always have behaved).

Impossible men: idle, illiterate,
    Self-pitying, dirty, sly,
For whose appearance even in City parks
    Excuses must be made to casual passers-by.

Has God's supply of tolerable husbands
    Fallen, in fact, so low?
Or do I always over-value woman
    At the expense of man?
              Do I?
                  It might be so.

ROBERT GRAVES

Because

Because the night you asked me,
the small scar of the quarter moon
had healed—the moon was whole again;
because life seemed so short;
because life stretched before me
like the darkened halls of nightmare;
because I knew exactly what I wanted;
because I knew exactly nothing;
because I shed my childhood with my clothes—
they both had years of wear left in them;
because your eyes were darker than my father's;
because my father said I could do better;
because I wanted badly to say no;
because Stanley Kowalski shouted "Stella . . .";
because you were a door I could slam shut;
because endings are written before beginnings;
because I knew that after twenty years
you'd bring the plants inside for winter
and make a jungle we'd sleep in naked;
because I had free will;
because everything is ordained;
I said yes.

LINDA PASTAN

A Prayer

because everyone knows exactly what's good for another
because very few see
because a man and a woman may just possibly look at each
    other
because in the insanity of human relationships there still
    may come a time we say: yes, yes
because a man or a woman can do anything he or she
    pleases
because you can reach any point in your life saying: now, i
    want this
because eventually it occurs we want each other, we want
    to know each other, even stupidly, even uglily
because there is at best a simple need in two people to try
    and reach some simple ground
because that simple ground is not so simple
because we are human beings gathered together whether
    we like it or not
because we are human beings reaching out to touch
because sometimes we grow
    we ask a blessing on this marriage
    we ask that some simplicity be allowed
    we ask their happiness
    we ask that this couple be known for what it is,
        and that the light shine upon it
    we ask a blessing for their marriage

JOEL OPPENHEIMER

from *The Prophet*

Then Almitra spoke again and said, And what of Marriage, master?
And he answered saying:
You were born together, and together you shall be for evermore.
You shall be together when the white wings of death scatter your
days.
Aye, you shall be together even in the silent memory of God.
But let there be spaces in your togetherness.
And let the winds of the heavens dance between you.

Love one another, but make not a bond of love:
Let it rather be a moving sea between the shores of your souls.
Fill each other's cup but drink not from one cup.
Give one another of your bread but eat not from the same loaf.
Sing and dance together and be joyous, but let each one of you be
alone,
Even as the strings of a lute are alone though they quiver with the
same music.
Give your hearts, but not into each other's keeping.
For only the hand of Life can contain your hearts.
And stand together yet not too near together:
For the pillars of the temple stand apart,
And the oak tree and the cypress grow not in each other's shadow.

KAHLIL GIBRAN

II

Epithalamia

Marriage Morning

Light, so low upon earth,
    You send a flash to the sun.
Here is the golden close of love,
    All my wooing is done.
Oh, the woods and the meadows,
    Woods where we hid from the wet,
Stiles where we stay'd to be kind,
    Meadows in which we met!

Light, so low in the vale,
    You flash and lighten afar,
For this is the golden morning of love,
    And you are his morning star.
Flash, I am coming, I come,
    By meadow and stile and wood,
Oh, lighten into my eyes and heart,
    Into my heart and my blood!

Heart, are you great enough
    For a love that never tires?
O heart, are you great enough for love?
    I have heard of thorns and briers.
Over the thorns and briers,
    Over the meadows and stiles,
Over the world to the end of it
    Flash for a million miles.

ALFRED, LORD TENNYSON

O Bride

O Bride brimful of
rosy little loves!

O brightest jewel of
the Queen of Paphos!

Come now
            to your
bedroom to your
bed
    and play there
sweetly   gently
with your bridegroom

And may Hesperus
lead you not at all
unwilling
            until

you stand wondering
before the silver

Throne of Hera
Queen of Marriage

SAPPHO,
translation by Mary Barnard

from *Epithalamion*

Open the temple gates unto my love,
Open them wide that she may enter in,
And all the postes adorne as doth behove,
And all the pillours deck with girlands trim,
For to recyve this Saynt with honour dew,
That commeth in to you.
With trembling steps and humble reverence,
She commeth in, before th'almighties vew,
Of her ye virgins learne obedience,
When so ye come into those holy places,
To humble your proud faces:
Bring her up to th'high altar, that she may
The sacred ceremonies there partake,
The which do endless matrimony make,
And let the roring Organs loudly play
The praises of the Lord in lively notes,
The whiles with hollow throates
The Choristers the joyous Antheme sing,
That al the woods may answere and their eccho ring.

Behold whiles she before the altar stands
Hearing the holy priest that to her speakes
And blesseth her with his two happy hands,
How the red roses flush up in her cheekes,
And the pure snow with goodly vermill stayne,
Like crimsin dyde in grayne,
That even th'Angels which continually,
About the sacred Altare doe remaine,
Forget their service and about her fly;
Ofte peeping in her face that seemes more fayre,
The more they on it stare.
But her sad eyes still fastened on the ground,
Are governed with goodly modesty,
That suffers not one looke to glaunce awry,
Which may let in a little thought unsownd.
Why blush ye love to give to me your hand,
The pledge of all our band?
Sing ye sweet Angels, Alleluya sing,
That all the woods may answere and your eccho ring.

(break)

Now al is done; bring home the bride againe,
Bring home the triumph of our victory,
Bring home with you the glory of her gaine,
With joyance bring her and with jollity.
Never had man more joyfull day then this,
Whom heaven would heape with blis.
Make feast therefore now all this live long day,
This day for ever to me holy is,
Poure out the wine without restraint or stay,
Poure not by cups, but by the belly full,
Poure out to all that wull,
And sprinkle all the postes and wals with wine,
That they may sweat, and drunken be withall.
Crowne ye God Bacchus with a coronall,
And Hymen also crowne with wreathes of vine,
And let the Graces daunce unto the rest;
For they can doo it best:
The whiles the maydens doe theyr carroll sing,
To which the woods shal answer and theyr eccho ring.

EDMUND SPENSER

Epithalamion

Singing, today I married my white girl
beautiful in a barley field.
Green on thy finger a grass blade curled,
so with this ring I thee wed, I thee wed,
and send our love to the loveless world
of all the living and all the dead.

Now, no more than vulnerable human,
we, more than one, less than two,
are nearly ourselves in a barley field—
and only love is the rent that's due
though the bailiffs of time return anew
to all the living but not the dead.

Shipwrecked, the sun sinks down harbours
of a sky, unloads its liquid cargoes
of marigolds, and I and my white girl
lie still in the barley—who else wishes
to speak, what more can be said
by all the living against all the dead?

Come then all you wedding guests:
green ghosts of trees, gold of barley,
you blackbird priests in the field,
you wind that shakes the pansy head
fluttering on a stalk like a butterfly;
come the living and come the dead.

Listen flowers, birds, winds, worlds,
tell all today that I married
more than a white girl in the barley—
for today I took to my human bed
flower and bird and wind and world,
and all the living and all the dead.

DANNIE ABSE

Epithalamium: The Single Light

Just as *coitus* means, really, *to travel together,*
this trip, this movement away from the self
toward the self, this deep delirium of cross-
purposes and unsheathed desires is a journey too:
treacherous, magical, serious, yet also a kind
of substantial gaiety, a dance in which the partners
embrace, separate, and return again to a single
place, in which the other-image ventures out
toward its partner, whom it finds, alters, is
altered by and renews, as wind and sycamore
alter, rectify and renew each other; as the slow,
unalterable turning of the earth alters the galaxies
in some way beyond our seeing. But what are
journeys for, if not to change the very urge that
moves them to begin? And what's marriage if not
a going out that quiets as it moves? Oh, someone
will always be wishing you luck, friends, but luck's
just choice made lucky by repeat, the way a man
thrown overboard makes his own life lucky by
the same stroke time and time again. Why, if I
were God, I'd let these glasses fill again with wine
and luck as Zeus did for that old pair whose only wish
was that they might burn, flicker and go out again
as a single flame. I'd make you oak and linden as
they were and call the shade a silence in your name.
I'd name the birds' embellished song for yours:
a noble thing, this word that's given as the word (the vow)
was meant to be, this utterance that love alone makes true,
its single light still burning in your eyes.

MICHAEL BLUMENTHAL

Epithalamium

In the streets the crowds go about their business
like they always do here, in the rain, or in the clear,
cold mornings before the shops close for the midday.

It is possible to do nothing but participate outside
along with everyone else, to look through the glass
and imagine unwrapping what is perfectly displayed.

They have lit small oil lamps the entire length
of the Via di Ripetta, where our rooms are ready for you.
The only information you need now is to know

that the walls are salmon-colored and there are carpets
to make the mornings easier to negotiate. The kitchen
is serviceable—enough for coffee and good toast.

We'll walk through the city that is so familiar to us;
the Piazza di Spagna with Keats' window at one o'clock,
the Caravaggios in San Luigi and the Piazza del Popolo,
and the *trattoria* sprinkled like parmigiano over the city.

I have alerted the notaries and the witnesses,
the officials at the Campidoglio and the embassy,
and the offices that will ask if there is anything

that speaks against what we're about to do. Even
the gold bands have been located in Via della Croce—
the time has come. I am waiting for you.

DANIEL HALPERN

They Came to the Wedding

Like gods who are fêted,
Like friendly old slaves,
Their silence full of music,
Their hands full of flowers,
Singly, in waves,
They came to the wedding.

First, sceptred with sunlight,
Slicing the shadows,
The Pharaoh came decked
In power, in sereneness
Like that of the lotus,
The lively, erect
Flower of forever.

The empress of China
Paraded her dragons
Of silver and gold,
While mountains were unloosing
Their hair to the music
Waterfalls trolled
Like bells for the wedding.

Saints came and sailors
With stories of marvels
And marvellous gifts,
And masts that now were branches
Broke into bird-song
Floating in drifts
Down branching horizons.

The deserts danced after,
The rivers before,
Till darkness like a mortal
Denying immortals
Thrust from the door
Those who came for the wedding.

BABETTE DEUTSCH

A Wedding Story

It was clear, sunny, and cold in New York
The day in November my sister,
Who was, after all, twenty-two,
Finally got married.
Just before the ceremony, Oswald was assassinated.
The TV was on as we left the house,
So we watched him get shot.
Then we drove off to the wedding.

There in the hall my grandfather sat
Muttering in a morose coat.
My father's good wool suit needed pressing,
And he'd forgotten his belt.
My mother was stacked into a gold dress.
Aunt Sylvia wore black.
Lynn, the bride, quivered in blue shantung.

With the Reform ceremony our side wasn't at home.
But Aunt Sylvia, my father's sister, wailed in Yiddish,
High and sweet, nodding and swaying,
Until all our valves were opened and lubricated.
Sylvia danced with my mother,
Ancient enemies musically moving,
Black and gold.
Following the armistice,
Everyone cheered and charged the buffet and ate gigantically.

When the dance band went at it,
Loud and Latin,
Aunt Sylvia sank her claws into my sleeve and spoke:
"Frankly, I don't feel normal.
I've spent my years alone, divorced, and now I'm almost old."
Focussing on her wasn't easy.
She peered at the dancers like a perturbed parrot,
Each eye outlined with primitive intensity,
Her nose a paler hue than the rest of her tropical face.

Aunt Sylvia left early,
But before she was gone she modelled the full-length mink
She had bought, she said, just for this affair,
With money she set aside from the years of her generous alimony.
Pointing to the coat,

And laughing tipsily toward his daughter, the bride,
Dad said to his new son-in-law,
"Make sure *she* gets one of those!"

"Let him lie in the earth where he belongs, for the sake of all Jews!"
My grandfather suddenly declared in Yiddish, referring to Oswald.
That really cleared the air
Of any lingering whiff of catastrophe.
The band began a hora,
Everyone rallied, forming one great circle,
In the center of which my father kicked
A kosatzke around my mother,
And in the center of the center
My mother shone and shook,
Wiggling her golden bottom,
Dancing off her goddam golden gong
While the whole wedding clapped
And jumped and carried on,
Beating the hell out of life
For the sake of the happy pair.

MELVIN WILK

A Wedding Toast

M. C. H.
C. H. W.
14 JULY 1971

St. John tells how, at Cana's wedding-feast,
The water-pots poured wine in such amount
That by his sober count
There were a hundred gallons at the least.

It made no earthly sense, unless to show
How whatsoever love elects to bless
Brims to a sweet excess
That can without depletion overflow.

Which is to say that what love sees is true;
That the world's fullness is not made but found.
Life hungers to abound
And pour its plenty out for such as you.

Now, if your loves will lend an ear to mine,
I toast you both, good son and dear new daughter.
May you not lack for water,
And may that water smack of Cana's wine.

RICHARD WILBUR

Witnessing a Wedding

Slowly and slower you have learned
to let yourselves grow while weaving
through each other in strong cloth.

It is not strangeness in the mate
you must fear, and not the fear
that loosens us so we lean back

chilly with a sudden draft on flesh
recently joined and taste again
the other sharp as tin in the mouth,

but familiarity we must mistrust,
the word based on the family
that fogs the sight and plugs the nose.

Fills the ears with the wax of possession.
Toughens the daily dead skin
callused against penetration.

Never think you know finally, or say
My husband likes, My wife is,
without balancing in the coil of the inner ear

that no one is surely anything till dead.
Love without respect is cold as a boa
constrictor, its caresses as choking.

Celebrate your differences in bed.
Like species, couples die out or evolve.
Ah strange new beasties with strawberry hides,

velvet green antlers, undulant necks,
tentacles, wings and the senses of bees,
your own changing mosaic of face

and the face of the stranger you live with
and try to love, who enters your body
like water, like pain, like food.

MARGE PIERCY

Epithalamion

FOR A SECOND MARRIAGE

If you, X, take this woman, Y,
and if you, Y, take this man, X,
you two who have taken each other
many times before, then this
is something to be trusted,

two separate folks not becoming halves,
as younger people do, but becoming
neither more nor less than yourselves,
separate *and* together, and if
this means a different kind of love,

as it must, if it means different
conveniences and inconveniences, as it must,
then let this *good luck*
from a friend act like grease
for what may yet be difficult, undefined,

and when the ordinary days of marriage
stretch out like prairie,
here's to the wisdom which understands
that if the heart's right
and the mind at ease with it

the prairie is a liveable place, a place
for withstanding all kinds of weather,
and here's to the little hills,
the ones that take you by surprise,
and the ones you'll need to invent.

STEPHEN DUNN

Upon a Second Marriage

FOR H. I. P.

Orchards, we linger here because
Women we love stand propped in your green prisons,
Obedient to such justly bending laws
    Each one longs to take root,
  Lives to confess whatever season's
Pride of blossom or endeavor's fruit
  May to her rustling boughs have risen.

Then autumn reddens the whole mind.
No more, she vows, the dazzle of a year
Shall woo her from your bare cage of loud wind,
    Promise the ring and run

  To burn the altar, reappear
With apple blossoms for the credulous one.
  Orchards, we wonder that we linger here!

  Orchards we planted, trees we shook
To learn what you were bearing, say we stayed
Because one winter dusk we half-mistook
    Frost on a bleakened bough
  For blossoms, and were half-afraid
To miss the old persuasion, should we go.
  And spring did come, and discourse made

  Enough of weddings to us all
That, loving her for whom the whole world grows
Fragrant and white, we linger to recall
    As down aisles of cut trees
  How a tall trunk's cross-section shows
Concentric rings, those many marriages
  That life on each live thing bestows.

JAMES MERRILL

The Wedding

When down I went to the rust-red quarry
I was informed, by birds, of your resolve
To live with me for ever and a day—
The day being always new and antecedent.
What could we ask of Nature? Nothing more
Than to outdo herself in our behalf.

Blossoms of caper, though they smell sweet,
Have never sailed the air like butterflies
Circling in innocent dance around each other
Over the cliff and out across the bay;
Nor has broom-blossom scorched a man's finger
With golden fire, kindled by sun.

Come, maids of honour and pages chosen
To attend this wedding, charged to perform
Incomparable feats—dance, caper-blossom!
Scorch, blossom of broom, our married fingers—
Though crowds of almost-men and almost-women
Howl for their lost immediacy.

ROBERT GRAVES

Omens

The whole day I kept looking
For omens. I thought sunshine
Would be a good sign, but rain
Is supposed to be O.K. too—
It was neither rainy nor sunny
But in-between, gray, not saying
Anything.

        I remember once
After a show we were walking
Out of the theater and I found
A dime on the sidewalk and saw
A shooting star a moment later
And figured the gods were saying:
"Marry her. Be happy forever."
But on the day of the wedding
There were no signs, just everyone
Crying, and the ambiguous weather.

The night before, alone
In a bed in my parents' house
I kept changing my mind. But flowers
Were ordered, gifts accepted, too late
To do anything but go through with it
And next morning I drove mechanically
Into the city, found a parking space
Exactly the size of my car (a sign?)
Went upstairs, opened the door
And saw her, dressed as a bride
Too beautiful to marry anyone.

I hung around the apartment
Only wanting the wedding to get
Going as planned. But when the last guests
Made it through the weekend traffic
And I stood under the canopy of flowers
The whole script I had written
Seemed wrong. I was supposed to say
"My love for you is an act of will"
But I could not say it
I could only stare at the sky
Light gray, neither rainy nor sunny
Above the jagged line of buildings.

(break)

During the party which followed
I got very tired standing up
And only wanted to drive to the hotel
And see how bad a mistake we'd made.
Our room overlooked the park. Skaters
Revolved on a patch of ice.
We sat in two chairs, drank
And stared out at the skyline
And didn't think about sex
Until she mentioned the best
Moment in the wedding was when
I couldn't say my lines
And up there, 26 floors high
"Radiating sanity and affection"
(As I described it in the ceremony)
Our love exploded like a rocket
And lit up the entire city.

ALAN FELDMAN

Wedding Day

I am afraid.
Sound has stopped in the day
And the images reel over
And over. Why all those tears,

The wild grief on his face
Outside the taxi? The sap
Of mourning rises
In our waving guests.

You sing behind the tall cake
Like a deserted bride
Who persists, demented,
And goes through the ritual.

When I went to the gents
There was a skewered heart
And a legend of love. Let me
Sleep on your breast to the airport.

SEAMUS HEANEY

The Wedding

The boys constructed
a wooden image of a bird.
It revolved on a pivot,
and it sang for us.

A musician played
a long horn,
though after the music was over,
we knew the horn would be broken
or buried.

My mother said:
name the first born
after the first person
who enters your house;

take the second one
up in your arms
as it cries, and rock it,
saying different names;

the name at which the child
stops crying
is the right one.

My father promised me
a new dress,
but that was not enough.

He promised me
a sway-backed horse, and said:
you have to be content with this.

I stood in the yard
waiting to leave;
the horse was stamping in the place
where the groom had passed . . .

My parents waved and called
Goodbye.

(break)

And as we left,
we could see the trees ahead
growing smaller,
the spaces between them
too narrow to go through.

MARCIA SOUTHWICK

Ark

The wooden coffer containing the tables of
the law kept in the Holiest Place of
the Tabernacle . . .

Oxford English Dictionary

FOR STEPHEN AND ELIZABETH

We all know
how the animals entered
that other ark
in twos,
even the promiscuous rooster
with his chosen hen,
even the snakes entwined,
remembering an earlier voyage
from Eden.
And Noah himself who knew
the worst of matrimony,
bitter words for breakfast,
complaints of sawdust
on the floor, nails underfoot;
at night her back turned,
hard and cold as the tablets.
Later the calls of mating
through the wet nights,
the tiny whir
of the hummingbirds' twin motors,
the monkeys' odd duet.
When the dove flew off
to find land
its mate perched on the railing,
the only creature
in that windy world alone.
I remember my wedding.
Standing before the ark
I thought of seas of matrimony,
of shipwreck.
When he stepped on the glass,
to recall the ruined temple, they say
I whispered: Man's dominion

over Woman. He smiled and shook his head
and later held a shard of glass
up to the light. In it
we saw condensed a perfect rainbow
and the white flash
of the dove's return.

LINDA PASTAN

Wreath for a Bridal

What though green leaves only witness
Such pact as is made once only; what matter
That owl voice sole 'yes', while cows utter
Low moos of approve; let sun surpliced in brightness
Stand stock still to laud these mated ones
Whose stark act all coming double luck joins.

Couched daylong in cloisters of stinging nettle
They lie, cut-grass assaulting each separate sense
With savor; coupled so, pure paragons of constance,
This pair seek single state from that dual battle.
Now speak some sacrament to parry scruple
For wedlock wrought within love's proper chapel.

Call here with flying colors all watchful birds
To people the twigged aisles; lead babel tongues
Of animals to choir: 'Look what thresh of wings
Wields guard of honor over these!' Starred with words
Let night bless that luck-rooted mead of clover
Where, bedded like angels, two burn one in fever.

From this holy day on, all pollen blown
Shall strew broadcast so rare a seed on wind
That every breath, thus teeming, set the land
Sprouting fruit, flowers, children most fair in legion
To slay spawn of dragon's teeth: speaking this promise,
Let flesh be knit, and each step hence go famous.

SYLVIA PLATH

Poem

FOR MARIE

Love, I shall perfect for you the child
Who diligently potters in my brain
Digging with heavy spade till sods were piled
Or puddling through muck in a deep drain.

Yearly I would sow my yard-long garden.
I'd strip a layer of sods to build the wall
That was to exclude sow and pecking hen.
Yearly, admitting these, the sods would fall.

Or in the sucking clabber I would splash
Delightedly and dam the flowing drain
But always my bastions of clay and mush
Would burst before the rising autumn rain.

Love, you shall perfect for me this child
Whose small imperfect limits would keep breaking:
Within new limits now, arrange the world
And square the circle: four walls and a ring.

SEAMUS HEANEY

Wedding-Wind

The wind blew all my wedding-day,
And my wedding-night was the night of the high wind;
And a stable door was banging, again and again,
That he must go and shut it, leaving me
Stupid in candlelight, hearing rain,
Seeing my face in the twisted candlestick,
Yet seeing nothing. When he came back
He said the horses were restless, and I was sad
That any man or beast that night should lack
The happiness I had.

                    Now in the day
All's ravelled under the sun by the wind's blowing.
He has gone to look at the floods, and I
Carry a chipped pail to the chicken-run,
Set it down, and stare. All is the wind
Hunting through clouds and forests, thrashing
My apron and the hanging cloths on the line.
Can it be borne, this bodying-forth by wind
Of joy my actions turn on, like a thread
Carrying beads? Shall I be let to sleep
Now this perpetual morning shares my bed?
Can even death dry up
These new delighted lakes, conclude
Our kneeling as cattle by all-generous waters?

Philip Larkin

Oh, Think Not I Am Faithful to a Vow!

Oh, think not I am faithful to a vow!
Faithless am I save to love's self alone.
Were you not lovely I would leave you now:
After the feet of beauty fly my own.
Were you not still my hunger's rarest food,
And water ever to my wildest thirst,
I would desert you—think not but I would!—
And seek another as I sought you first.
But you are mobile as the veering air,
And all your charms more changeful than the tide,
Wherefore to be inconstant is no care:
I have but to continue at your side.
So wanton, light and false, my love, are you,
I am most faithless when I most am true.

EDNA ST. VINCENT MILLAY

III

So Much Happiness

It Is Marvellous to Wake Up Together

It is marvellous to wake up together
At the same minute; marvellous to hear
The rain begin suddenly all over the roof,
To feel the air clear
As if electricity had passed through it
From a black mesh of wires in the sky.
All over the roof the rain hisses,
And below, the light falling of kisses.

An electrical storm is coming or moving away;
It is the prickling air that wakes us up.
If lightning struck the house now, it would run
From the four blue china balls on top
Down the roof and down the rods all around us,
And we imagine dreamily
How the whole house caught in a bird–cage of lightning
Would be quite delightful rather than frightening:

And from the same simplified point of view
Of night and lying flat on one's back
All things might change equally easily,
Since always to warn us there must be these black
Electrical wires dangling. Without surprise

The world might change to something quite different,
As the air changes or the lightning comes without our blinking.
Change as our kisses are changing without our thinking.

ELIZABETH BISHOP

7, 22, 66

Which doesn't belong in this group of three?—
Soap, Bible, stationery.
Two deal with creation;
So obviously the soap

Doesn't blend—
It can't wash away the fate
Of three of us trying to belong
To one another.

But on our honeymoon, from the key's first turn,
I thought the misfit was the Bible.
I was already with child
Beside the Gideon cover with its torch.

Fresh out of the shower, you judged each queen
For softness; I packed the stationery.
Even while we lay still,
Fog closed the window.

From the Port Townsend double on heavy pilings,
Tides grow barnacles and starfish
Under the bed, we did not take God's word
For a souvenir.

Rustling an atlas, catching the morning ferry,
You went on with me, into a life that had stolen you,
Asking that night for a decent room for two,
And puzzling out the number on its key.

SANDRA McPHERSON

Wishful Thinking

I like to think that ours will be more than just another story
of failed love and the penumbras of desire. I like to think
that the moon that day was in whatever house the astrologists
would have it in for a kind of quiet, a trellis lust could climb
easily and then subside, resting against the sills and ledges,
giving way like shore to an occasional tenderness, coddling
the cold idiosyncrasies of impulse and weather that pound it
as it holds to its shape against the winds and duststorms of
temptation and longing. I like to think that some small canister
of hope and tranquillity washed ashore that day and we, in
the right place, found it. These are the things I imagine
all lovers wish for amid the hot commencements of love
and promises, their histories and failures washing ashore
like flotsam, their innards girthed against those architects
of misery, desire and restlessness, their hope rising
against the air as it fondles the waves and frolics them skywards.
I like to think that, if the heart pauses awhile in a single place,
it finds a home somewhere, like a vagabond lured by fatigue
to an unlikely town and, with a sudden peacefulness, deciding
to stay there. I like to think these things because, whether
or not they reach fruition, they provide the heart with a kind
of solace, the way poetry does, or all forms of tenderness
that issue out amid the deserts of failed love and petulant desire.
I like to think them because, meditated on amid this pattern
of off-white and darkness, they lend themselves to a kind of
music, not unlike the music a dove makes as it circles the trees,
not unlike the sun and the earth and their orbital brothers,
the planets, as they chant to the heavens their longing for hope
and repetition amid orderly movement, not unlike the music
these humble wishes make with their cantata of willfulness
and good intentions, looking for some pleasant abstractions
amid our concretized lives, something tender and lovely to
defy the times with, quiet and palpable amid the flickers of flux
and the flames of longing: a bird rising over the ashes, a dream.

MICHAEL BLUMENTHAL

For Love

FOR BOBBIE

Yesterday I wanted to
speak of it, that sense above
the others to me
important because all

that I know derives
from what it teaches me.
Today, what is it that
is finally so helpless,

different, despairs of its own
statement, wants to
turn away, endlessly
to turn away.

If the moon did not . . .
no, if you did not
I wouldn't either, but
what would I not

do, what prevention, what
thing so quickly stopped.
That is love yesterday
or tomorrow, not

now. Can I eat
what you give me. I
have not earned it. Must
I think of everything

as earned. Now love also
becomes a reward so
remote from me I have
only made it with my mind.

Here is tedium,
despair, a painful
sense of isolation and
whimsical if pompous

(break)

self-regard. But that image
is only of the mind's
vague structure, vague to me
because it is my own.

Love, what do I think
to say. I cannot say it.
What have you become to ask,
what have I made you into,

companion, good company,
crossed legs with skirt, or
soft body under
the bones of the bed.

Nothing says anything
but that which it wishes
would come true, fears
what else might happen in

some other place, some
other time not this one.
A voice in my place, an
echo of that only in yours.

Let me stumble into
not the confession but
the obsession I begin with
now. For you

also (also)
some time beyond place, or
place beyond time, no
mind left to

say anything at all,
that face gone, now.
Into the company of love
it all returns.

ROBERT CREELEY

The Wife

A frog under you,
knees drawn up
ready to leap out of time,

a dog beside you,
snuffing at you, seeking
scent of you, an idea unformulated,

I give up on
trying to answer my question,
Do I love you enough?

It's enough to be
so much here. And
certainly when I catch

your mind in the
act of plucking
truth from the dark surrounding nowhere

as a swallow skims a
gnat from the
deep sky,

I don't stop to ask myself
Do I love him? but
laugh for joy.

DENISE LEVERTOV

The Skunk

Up, black, striped and demasked like the chasuble
At a funeral Mass, the skunk's tail
Paraded the skunk. Night after night
I expected her like a visitor.

The refrigerator whinnied into silence.
My desk light softened beyond the verandah.
Small oranges loomed in the orange tree.
I began to be tense as a voyeur.

After eleven years I was composing
Love-letters again, broaching the word 'wife'
Like a stored cask, as if its slender vowel
Had mutated into the night earth and air

Of California. The beautiful, useless
Tang of eucalyptus spelt your absence.
The aftermath of a mouthful of wine
Was like inhaling you off a cold pillow.

And there she was, the intent and glamorous,
Ordinary, mysterious skunk,
Mythologized, demythologized,
Snuffing the boards five feet beyond me.

It all came back to me last night, stirred
By the sootfall of your things at bedtime,
Your head-down, tail-up hunt in a bottom drawer
For the black plunge-line nightdress.

SEAMUS HEANEY

So Much Happiness

FOR MICHAEL

It is difficult to know what to do with so much happiness.
With sadness there is something to rub against,
a wound to tend with lotion and cloth.
When the world falls in around you, you have pieces to pick up,
something to hold in your hands, like ticket stubs or change.

But happiness floats.
It doesn't need you to hold it down.
It doesn't need anything.
Happiness lands on the roof of the next house, singing,
and disappears when it wants to.
You are happy either way.
Even the fact that you once lived in a peaceful tree house
and now live over a quarry of noise and dust
cannot make you unhappy.
Everything has a life of its own,
it too could wake up filled with possibilities
of coffee cake and ripe peaches,
and love even the floor which needs to be swept,
the soiled linens and scratched records . . .

Since there is no place large enough
to contain so much happiness,
you shrug, you raise your hands, and it flows out of you
into everything you touch. You are not responsible.
You take no credit, as the night sky takes no credit
for the moon, but continues to hold it, and share it,
and in that way, be known.

NAOMI SHIHAB NYE

The Blind Leading the Blind

Take my hand. There are two of us in this cave.
The sound you hear is water; you will hear it forever.
The ground you walk on is rock. I have been here before.
People come here to be born, to discover, to kiss,
to dream and to dig and to kill. Watch for the mud.
Summer blows in with scent of horses and roses;
fall with the sound of sound breaking; winter shoves
its empty sleeve down the dark of your throat.
You will learn toads from diamonds, the fist from the palm,
love from the sweat of love, falling from flying.
There are a thousand turnoffs. I have been here before.
Once I fell off a precipice. Once I found gold.
Once I stumbled on murder, the thin parts of a girl.
Walk on, keep walking, there are axes above us.
Watch for occasional bits and bubbles of light—
birthdays for you, recognitions: *yourself, another.*
Watch for the mud. Listen for bells, for beggars.
Something with wings went crazy against my chest once.
There are two of us here. Touch me.

Lisel Mueller

Domestic Song

In the space of my life I design such rooms:
I trim the air to music's measurements; I start
a fire in the fire's place; you are secure
in the double-chambered neighborhood
of loving, and the whole house raises
its cain of distinct
possibilities. Let us
have our differences: let go

wildness from its hold, the buzz and heat
of pleasure from its separate cells. The sweetness
is of paradox, intact, untouched, in the couch
of an accommodating hearth, in the nightlong
red-hot beehive we have started.

HEATHER McHUGH

Primitive

I have heard about the civilized,
the marriages run on talk, elegant and
honest, rational. But you and I are
savages. You come in with a bag,
hold it out to me in silence.
I know Moo Shu Pork when I smell it
and understand the message: I have
pleased you greatly last night. We sit
quietly, side by side, to eat,
the long pancakes dangling and spilling,
fragrant sauce dripping out,
and glance at each other askance, wordless,
the corners of our eyes clear as spear points
laid along the sill to show
a friend sits with a friend here.

SHARON OLDS

Poem to My Husband from My Father's Daughter

I have always admired your courage. As I see you
embracing me, in the mirror, I see I am
my father as a woman, I see you bravely
embrace him in me, putting your life in his
hands as mine. You know who I am—you can
see his hair springing from my head like
oil from the ground, you can see his eyes,
reddish as liquor left in a shot-glass and
dried dark, looking out of my face,
and his firm sucking lips, and the breasts
rising frail as blisters from his chest,
tipped with apple-pink. You are fearless, you
enter him as a woman, my sex like a
wound in his body, you flood your seed in his
life as me, you entrust your children to that
man as a mother, his hands as my hands
cupped around their tiny heads. I have never
known a man with your courage, coming
naked into the cage with the lion, I
lay my enormous paws on your scalp I
take my great tongue and begin to
run the rasp delicately
along your skin, humming: as you enter
ecstasy, the hairs lifting
all over your body, I have never seen a
happier man.

SHARON OLDS

Cherish

From the window I see her bend to the roses
holding close to the bloom so as not to
prick her fingers. With the other hand she clips, pauses and
clips, more alone in the world
than I had known. She won't
look up, not now. She's alone
with roses and with something else I can only think, not
say. I know the names of those bushes

given for our late wedding: Love, Honor, Cherish—
this last the rose she holds out to me suddenly, having
entered the house between glances. I press
my nose to it, draw the sweetness in, let it cling—scent
of promise, of treasure. My hand on her wrist to bring her close,
her eyes green as river-moss. Saying it then, against
what comes: *wife,* while I can, while my breath, each hurried petal
can still find her.

RAYMOND CARVER

from *That Walk Away as One: A Marriage Brood*

This afternoon I came up the stairs from the subway
at the southwest corner of Broadway and 96th Street
at the exact same moment you were striding
north on that corner. Tall; dark overcoat—
it's false to put together
recalled details, as if I'd seen a stranger.
How then to remember and separate what I saw?
It was you. Pure pleasure in recognition
doesn't say it either. There you were
so simply before my eyes and walking fast
and a split second later you saw me too.
A gift, a gift! Did we kiss? I took your arm,
we hardly missed a beat, we crossed the street
and did our errands—wine, squid, number one
pencils, grapefruit—went home; went on living.

This walking arm in arm in harmony
having come from separate directions—
this is marriage too. It looks so easy
and is perhaps so easy and is not.
It always is a gift.
It gives a form to life
perhaps invisibly. I don't look married.

RACHEL HADAS

IV

Toward a Definition of Marriage

from *Solomon and the Witch*

For though love has a spider's eye
To find out some appropriate pain—
Aye, though all passion's in the glance—
For every nerve, and tests a lover
With cruelties of Choice and Chance;
And when at last that murder's over
Maybe the bride-bed brings despair,
For each an imagined image brings
And finds a real image there;
Yet the world ends when these two things,
Though several, are a single light,
When oil and wick are burned in one;
Therefore a blessed moon last night
Gave Sheba to her Solomon.

WILLIAM BUTLER YEATS

from *Toward a Definition of Marriage*

I

It is to make a fill, not find a land.
Elsewhere, often, one sights americas of awareness,
suddenly there they are, natural and anarchic,
with plantings scattered but rich, powers to be harnessed—
but this is more like building a World's Fair island.
Somebody thought it could be done, contracts are signed,
and now all materials are useful, everything; sludge
is scooped up and mixed with tin cans and fruit rinds,
even tomato pulp and lettuce leaves are solid
under pressure. Presently the ground humps up and shows.
But this marvel of engineering is not all.
A hodgepodge of creatures (no bestiary would suppose
such an improbable society) are at this time
turned loose to run on it, first shyly, then more free,
and must keep, for self's sake, wiles, anger, much of their
spiney or warted nature, yet learn courtesy.

V

Say, for once, that the start is a pure vision
like the blind man's (though he couldn't keep it, trees
soon bleached to familiar) when the bandage came off
and what a world could be first fell on his eyes.
Say it's when campaigns are closest to home
that farsighted lawmakers oftenest lose their way.
And repeat what everyone knows and nobody wants
to remember, that always, always expediency
must freckle the fairest wishes. Say, when documents,
stiff with history, go right into the council chambers
and are rolled up to shake under noses, are constantly read from,
or pounded on, or passed around, the parchment limbers;
and, still later, if these old papers are still being shuffled,
commas will be missing, ashes will disfigure a word;
finally thumbprints will grease out whole phrases, the clear prose
won't mean much; it can never be wholly restored.
Curators mourn the perfect idea, for it crippled
outside of its case. Announce that at least it can move
in the imperfect action, beyond the windy oratory,
of marriage, which is the politics of love.

MONA VAN DUYN

Marriage

There could be a good husband
and a good wife and a bad marriage
all in one, a woman thinking
she could have this or have that,
a man infected with the latest idea
or the other wanting nothing
or wanting each other but at separate
times when the other's loneliness
is not clawing, it is more fantastic
than charting the many ships
and planes coming into the busiest
harbor or port, this business
of the man and woman somehow
landing together, somehow managing
another flight, right on schedule.
And what a port!—sometimes in high
winds not just planes, ships but
balloons, dirigibles, kites, trucks,
covered wagons, all to be secured.

DAVID RAY

Tree Marriage

In Chota Nagpur and Bengal
the betrothed are tied with threads to
mango trees, they marry the trees
as well as one another, and
the two trees marry each other.
Could we do that some time with oaks
or beeches? This gossamer we
hold each other with, this web
of love and habit is not enough.
In mistrust of heavier ties,
I would like tree-siblings for us,
standing together somewhere, two
trees married with us, lightly, their
fingers barely touching in sleep,
our threads invisible but holding.

WILLIAM MEREDITH

A Bride Again

When I am a bride again
I will carry water
lilies and at the altar
there will be three urns,
one of ash
another of air
and the third will be of earth.

There will be no water
for the lilies or for me.
We will move in an arid dream
of white dust and lace, a ritual
nightmare in which all
the solitude and sway of our long
stems will be broken
again.

I will lift my veil
and the lilies will close
for there is no water
in marriage, only blood.

SUSAN KINSOLVING

Marriage

We are waiting in separate rooms
with doors closed between us.
In the desire to be apart is the wish
to renew ourselves to each other
and so we sit each alone
with nothing to do, really,
for we are all there is to do,
our rooms silent.
                    We listen
to boys in the street
boisterous on a night out.

Our life together has been to shore up good
against evil, to keep us from being flooded apart,
to keep land beneath us: to stem the onrush
of more evil mounting with spite of guilt;
to place a soft wall, evil subsiding against it
in sleep, reproachful sleep that turns
to flowered dreams breathing deeply upon softness.
And we have succeeded, by being a wall to each
          other,
to keep us from flooding ourselves with the fiery
and omnivorous.
                    We wave to one another
from the ramparts,
with no man's land between.

You sat across the table and drew pictures,
perhaps of me or of others with us;
you cannot recall, here now bound to me
in marriage. With such mystery is time filled.

I approached from around the table,
smiling, my curiosity to this day
unfilled. What did we do to bring us
together, you smiling at me in return?
A mystery in which we are held
side by side, because it cannot be answered
by a few phrases about love.

(break)

I lie here, my thoughts restful
as if life were moving to some haven,
and getting up to find food
for my stomach with the passing hours,
I say, protesting to myself,
But I have lived.

DAVID IGNATOW

Love and Memory

In those days the sky hung like a cobweb
In the great garden of space. There were faces
In water, as though the river were trying
On its own to evolve. Now after years

Of telling each other apart, love
Is not born spontaneously, but is realized
In the brain or in the arms almost
Mathematically. There are words

That lose courage when you speak them,
Even in the darkest room of the house,
To a wife who waits for a single face
To emerge from collective rhythms. Who can argue

With marriage, you believe, for marriage
Is a long novel of associations, specks of gold
Swept by on a long river. Where it leads
Is to memory, the odor of lemon trees

After a storm, and the way blood clots around a cut
Leads you further back to those days
In the mountains where air was so transparent
You both consulted stars. But memories,

In bed in the dark, are fictitious characters,
And a common past does not mean
Memories in common. Everyone tells lies in bed
And you are almost certain

You have met this woman before,
Or this is a dream: into the earth
Crushed flowers have been pressed,
And you walk out on them

As though you were resuming an old habit.
A memory passes over you, odor of lemons
In a bath, pearly skin, the dark, dark hair.
A memory of what world? What life?

STEVE ORLEN

Mathematics of Love

The links are chance, the chain is fate,
Constricting as Hephaistos' net
Which to the smiles of gods betrayed
Two bodies on a single bed,
So tightly knit, the truth was plain:
One multiplied by one is one.

Subtracting lovers who retort
That what chance coupled, choice can part
(As if mere effort could relax
The clutches of a paradox)
At last to their amazement find
Themselves the dwindled dividend,

Deep in that hell where Don Juan
Knows he has added names in vain
Since all the aggregate is lost
To him, not widowed but a ghost,
While those bereaved of one possess
A minus greater than his plus.

True love begins with algebra,
Those casual actors x and y,
Nonentities whose magic role
Is to turn nothing into all,
To be and not to be, to mate:
The links are chance, the chain is fate.

MICHAEL HAMBURGER

To My Wife

19 MARCH 1951

Choice of you shuts up that peacock-fan
The future was, in which temptingly spread
All that elaborative nature can.
Matchless potential! but unlimited
Only so long as I elected nothing;
Simply to choose stopped all ways up but one,
And sent the tease-birds from the bushes flapping.
No future now. I and you now, alone.

So for your face I have exchanged all faces,
For your few properties bargained the brisk
Baggage, the mask-and-magic-man's regalia.
Now you become my boredom and my failure,
Another way of suffering, a risk,
A heavier-than-air hypostasis.

PHILIP LARKIN

Most Like an Arch This Marriage

Most like an arch—an entrance which upholds
and shores the stone-crush up the air like lace.
Mass made idea, and idea held in place.
A lock in time. Inside half-heaven unfolds.

Most like an arch—two weaknesses that lean
into a strength. Two fallings become firm.
Two joined abeyances become a term
naming the fact that teaches fact to mean.

Not quite that? Not much less. World as it is,
what's strong and separate falters. All I do
at piling stone on stone apart from you
is roofless around nothing. Till we kiss

I am no more than upright and unset.
It is by falling in and in we make
the all-bearing point, for one another's sake,
in faultless failing, raised by our own weight.

JOHN CIARDI

Marriage

No wandering any more where the feet stumble
Upon a sudden rise, or sink in damp
Marsh grasses. No uncertain following on
With nothing there to follow—a sure bird,
A fence, a farmhouse. No adventuring now
Where motion that is yet not motion dies.
Circles have lost their magic, and the voice
Comes back upon itself. . . . The road is firm.
It runs, and the dust is not too deep, and the end
Never can heave in sight—though one is there.
It runs in a straight silence, till a word
Turns it; then a sentence, and evening falls
At an expected inn, whose barest room
Cannot be lonely if a hand is reached
To touch another hand, the walls forgotten. . . .
Laughter is morning, and the road resumes;
Adventurous, it never will return.

MARK VAN DOREN

A Marriage

FOR MARGIE SMIGEL AND JON DOPKEEN

You are holding up a ceiling
with both arms. It is very heavy,
but you must hold it up, or else
it will fall down on you. Your arms
are tired, terribly tired,
and, as the day goes on, it feels
as if either your arms or the ceiling
will soon collapse.

But then,
unexpectedly,
something wonderful happens:
Someone,
a man or a woman,
walks into the room
and holds their arms up
to the ceiling beside you.

So you finally get
to take down your arms.
You feel the relief of respite,
the blood flowing back
to your fingers and arms.
And when your partner's arms tire,
you hold up your own
to relieve him again.

And it can go on like this
for many years
without the house falling.

MICHAEL BLUMENTHAL

The Common Wisdom

Their marriage is a good one. In our eyes
What makes a marriage *good?* Well, that the tether
Fray but not break, and that they stay together.
One should be watching while the other dies.

HOWARD NEMEROV

Domestic Interior

FOR KEVIN

The woman is as round
as the new ring
ambering her finger.
The mirror weds her.
She has long since been bedded.

There is
about it all
a quiet search for attention,
like the unexpected shine
of a despised utensil.

The oils,
the varnishes,
the cracked light,
the worm of permanence—
all of them supplied by Van Eyck—

by whose edict she will stay
burnished, fertile
on her wedding day,
interred in her joy.
Love, turn.

The convex of your eye
that is so loving, bright
and constant yet shows
only this woman in her varnishes,
who won't improve in the light.

But there's a way of life
that is its own witness:
put the kettle on, shut the blind.
Home is a sleeping child,
an open mind

and our effects,
shrugged and settled
in the sort of light
jugs and kettles
grow important by.

EAVAN BOLAND

V

Two-Part Harmony

from *The Country of Marriage*

3.

Sometimes our life reminds me
of a forest in which there is a graceful clearing
and in that opening a house,
an orchard and garden,
comfortable shades, and flowers
red and yellow in the sun, a pattern
made in the light for the light to return to.
The forest is mostly dark, its ways
to be made anew day after day, the dark
richer than the light and more blessed,
provided we stay brave
enough to keep on going in.

4.

How many times have I come to you out of my head
with joy, if ever a man was,
for to approach you I have given up the light
and all directions. I come to you
lost, wholly trusting as a man who goes
into the forest unarmed. It is as though I descend
slowly earthward out of the air. I rest in peace
in you, when I arrive at last.

6.

What I am learning to give you is my death
to set you free of me, and me from myself
into the dark and the new light. Like the water
of a deep stream, love is always too much. We
did not make it. Though we drink till we burst
we cannot have it all, or want it all.
In its abundance it survives our thirst.
In the evening we come down to the shore
to drink our fill, and sleep, while it
flows through the regions of the dark.
It does not hold us, except we keep returning
to its rich waters thirsty. We enter,
willing to die, into the commonwealth of its joy.

(break)

7.

I give you what is unbounded, passing from dark to dark,
containing darkness: a night of rain, an early morning.
I give you the life I have let live for love of you:
a clump of orange-blooming weeds beside the road,
the young orchard waiting in the snow, our own life
that we have planted in this ground, as I
have planted mine in you. I give you my love for all
beautiful and honest women that you gather to yourself
again and again, and satisfy—and this poem,
no more mine than any man's who has loved a woman.

WENDELL BERRY

Homecoming

Having come unto
the tall house of our habit
where it settles rump downward
on its stone foundations
in the manner of a homely brood mare
who throws good colts

and having entered
where sunlight is pasted on the windows
ozone rises from the mullions
dust motes pollinate the hallway
and spiders remembering a golden age
sit one in each drain

we will hang up our clothes and our vegetables
we will decorate the rafters with mushrooms
on our hearth we will burn splits of silver popple
we will stand up to our knees in their flicker
the soup kettle will clang five notes of pleasure
and love will take up quarters.

MAXINE KUMIN

Habitation

Marriage is not
a house or even a tent

it is before that, and colder:

the edge of the forest, the edge
of the desert
                    the unpainted stairs
at the back where we squat
outside, eating popcorn

the edge of the receding glacier

where painfully and with wonder
at having survived even
this far

we are learning to make fire

MARGARET ATWOOD

Song for a Marriage

Housed in each other's arms,
Thatched with each other's grace,
Your bodies, flint on steel
Striking out fire to fend
The cold away awhile;
With sweat for mortar, brace
Your walls against the sleet
And the rib-riddling wind.

A house, you house yourselves,
Housed, you will house another,
Scaled to a subtler blueprint
Than architects can draw—
A triple function yours
In this world's winter weather,
Oh, breathing brick and stone,
I look on you with awe.

A fig for praise that calls
Flesh a bundle of sticks,
Kindling for flame that feels
Like swallowing the sun!
Yet luxury turned labor's
No old maid's rancid mix,
But how bone-masonry
Outweighs the skeleton.

VASSAR MILLER

A Marriage

Diving nude into the pond they made—
the woman first, then the man.
Their dog barks. I am the friend,
I've come up the long driveway with my bottles of wine, good bread,
            my persistent need for their table.

My friends swim slowly back and forth across the pond
            across the diminishing shafts of light
lingering, lingering, like people at a table, unable
to let go. The good black-and-white dog shakes himself dry.

There is a sadness in our quiet walk
to the house, in the way he reminds her of some small chore
they must do after dinner. The dog finds her hand
and her palm rests on his spotted head. I watch them, loving them,
loving this trilogy of faithfulness renewing itself
with each attention to one thing, and the next.

ROBIN BECKER

from *The One Day*

Smoke rises all day from two chimneys above us.
You stand by the stove looking south, through bare branches
of McIntosh, Spy, and Baldwin. You add oak logs
to the fire you built at six in the castiron stove.
At the opposite end of the same house, under another chimney,
I look toward the pond that flattens to the west
under the low sun of a January afternoon, from a notebook
busy with bushels and yields. All day in our opposite
rooms we carry wood to stoves, we pace up and down, we plan,
we set figures on paper—to converge at day's end

for kisses, bread, and talk; then we read in silence,
sitting in opposite chairs; then we turn drowsy.
Dreaming of tomorrow only, we sleep in the painted bed
while the night's frail twisting of woodsmoke assembles
overhead from the two chimneys, to mingle and disperse
as our cells will disperse and mingle when they lapse
into graveyard dirt. Meantime the day is double
in the work, love, and solitude of eyes
that gaze not at each other but at a third thing:
a child, a ciderpress, a book—work's paradise.

DONALD HALL

Two-Part Harmony

A little piccolo and wheezy oboe
signal the start of my new day.
It's Martha snoring in early morning.

> Like singing to the gently rolling sea,
> Singing in the morning to Martha
> Is like singing the best two-part harmony.

It's Martha making water.
She gropes back to bed, eyes shut tight
to extend that sleep-sense she so adores,
but I have long ago rearranged her life,
her pillow tucked-in tight like a body.

"Oh, Chrismas sakes, honestly, shush, shush, shs . . ."

> She loves my break-of-dawn jocularity.
> Singing in the morning to Martha,
> Lying sturdy next to me.

Hello, what's that new song
taped to the refrigerator door?

"Morning cheerfulness, the principal cause
of husband beating."

> You can tell that we agree,
> Singing in the morning,
> Singing la-de-da, Martha and me.

PETER KAROFF

Love Song: I and Thou

Nothing is plumb, level, or square:
   the studs are bowed, the joists
are shaky by nature, no piece fits
   any other piece without a gap
or pinch, and bent nails
   dance all over the surfacing
like maggots. By Christ
   I am no carpenter. I built
the roof for myself, the walls
   for myself, the floors
for myself, and got
   hung up in it myself. I
danced with a purple thumb
   at this house-warming, drunk
with my prime whiskey: rage.
   Oh I spat rage's nails
into the frame-up of my work:
   it held. It settled plumb,
level, solid, square and true
   for that great moment. Then
it screamed and went on through,
   skewing as wrong the other way.
God damned it. This is hell,
   but I planned it, I sawed it,
I nailed it, and I
   will live in it until it kills me.
I can nail my left palm
   to the left-hand crosspiece but
I can't do everything myself.
   I need a hand to nail the right,
a help, a love, a you, a wife.

ALAN DUGAN

The Night the Children Were Away

When she comes home he's waiting for her
on the secluded deck, naked,
the wine open,

her favorite cheese already sliced.
Though he hasn't done anything
like this in years

he knows she'll laugh at his nakedness
as one laughs at seeing
an old friend

at a dirty movie. Then she'll take off
her clothes, join him.
Tonight

he wants to make love profanely
as if the profane
were the only way

to disturb, to waken, the sacred.
But neither is in a hurry.
They sip wine,

touch a little, nothing much needs
to be said. That glacial
intolerable drift

toward quietude and habit, he was worried
that he'd stopped worrying
about it.

It's time, a kiss says, to stop time
by owning it, transforming it
into body-time, hip-sway

and heartbeat, though really the kiss says
now, the now he trusts
is both history

and this instant, reflexive, the good past
brought forward in a rush.

STEPHEN DUNN

After Making Love We Hear Footsteps

For I can snore like a bullhorn
or play loud music
or sit up talking with any reasonably sober Irishman
and Fergus will only sink deeper
into his dreamless sleep, which goes by all in one flash,
but let there be that heavy breathing
or a stifled come-cry anywhere in the house
and he will wrench himself awake
and make for it on the run—as now, we lie together,
after making love, quiet, touching along the length of our bodies,
familiar touch of the long-married,
and he appears—in his baseball pajamas, it happens,
the neck opening so small
he has to screw them on, which one day may make him wonder
about the mental capacity of baseball players—
and flops down between us and hugs us and snuggles himself to sleep,
his face gleaming with satisfaction at being this very child.

In the half darkness we look at each other
and smile
and touch arms across his little, startlingly muscled body—
this one whom habit of memory propels to the ground of his making,
sleeper only the mortal sounds can sing awake,
this blessing love gives again into our arms.

GALWAY KINNELL

You Hold Me in My Life

You hold me in my life you breathe my breath
My fingertips ignite within your shade
Within your shade there flares my little death
Whose held unmaking holds what you have made

Flesh of my flesh we kindle to a choice
It is a stone a cell of blood a child
Its voice is rising burning in your voice
And sings within my throat a little while

Bone of my bone you hold me in my flame
I am a burning voice a child a stone
Within your cell I sing our own child's name
And as he rises I lie down alone

Alone my body and my world with you
We leave our blessing though all deaths burn true

ROBERT PACK

The Message

When you appeared in my dream
with your eyes blackened,
I knew it was a sign.

I knew I had understood
the secret of your illness,
your sudden collapse, your screams
and doubled-over frailty,
your youthful face blotted, only
a pale drained mask in its place.

I knew my own body was as vulnerable,
that what we call Getting Older
is really an uncovering,
the delicate inner shell revealed.

This thought drove the life
from me and I joined you on the bed
where you rested, my life companion.
And I held you in my sudden weakness,
clinging to your bare legs and your
narrow back, breathing your warm neck
and your hair.

       It was then,
at our closest—our weakest—
I knew nothing less than death
could break us, that death wouldn't
break us.

CHARLES FISHMAN

VI

Identities

This Blessing

FOR ISABELLE

Last night I turned in the bed to find you
and you were there, with your body of deep light
and a third heartbeat beating inside you.
I didn't know what to do, out of hunger
and gratitude, so I merely held you,
body that was not my body, scent
that was not my scent, soul
that was not my soul, and listened
to the mixed angels of sleep and oblivion
as they sang in the traffic of the bewitching hours.
I went to hold you, as lovers who have woken
to their own, explicable sadness will,
and felt you, entirely other and entwined,
seed to my seed, breath to my breath, dreams
spiraling to meet my dreams. *Who has not wept*
that love can offer us so little? And wept again
that it can do so much? Turning away from you
once more, I enfolded myself again in the sleep
of my own wisdom, its love and its hate,
its pain and its pleasure,
its merely human blessing: this sadness,
this sweetness.

MICHAEL BLUMENTHAL

Identities

When I reached the sea
I fell in with another who had just come
From the interior. Her family
Had figured in a past regime
But her father was now imprisoned.

She had travelled, only by night,
Escaping just as her own warrant
Arrived and stealing the police boat,
As far as this determined coast.

As it happened, we were staying at the same
Hotel, pink and goodish for the tourist
Quarter. She came that evening to my room
Asking me to go to the capital,
Offering me wristwatch and wallet,
To search out an old friend who would steal
Papers for herself and me. Then to be married,
We could leave from that very harbour.

I have been wandering since, back up the streams
That had once flowed simply one into the other,
One taking the other's name.

PAUL MULDOON

Driving Home in Two Cars

This moon isn't like some other thing—
just a moon, four or five days old,
but bright enough I've got to squint to see it all.
I look a second time, then back to the road
to find the car I'm following is gone.

Down through foothills,
not knowing the way home,
I imagine the baby sagging toward her thumb,
my husband turning back to talk to our son,
radio yawning and sputtering on as their
wheels slip an embankment . . .

I gun the engine
round three curves
and nearly rear-end them.
Out of breath, we start again.

Not porchlights, not nightlights,
just taillights: still
I train my half-sad love
on these red points.
An old van passes,
slips briefly inbetween,

as if nothing joins us.
Near dawn one night, unable to sleep,
I tracked my husband
breath for breath,
determined to catch up.
And though I couldn't,
though I didn't,
I wouldn't give up until he woke.

Listening to our children
whirring in their beds—distinct
from each other, distinct
from us—I've wished away their bodies,
wished away our own,
as if that would bring us home.

(break)

This is almost it:
a year-old boy opens a book
to his favorite page
(magic to him, magic to him),
sets it on the floor,
stands on it,
waits,
then breaks into tears.

Farmhouses with Christmas trees
stream on the periphery,
the moon starts its slide
down a slough of stars.

I watch the taillights of our car.

JODY BOLZ

Ways of Looking at a Wife

The motion is always swift, always unexpected.
The great, gangling, gawking heron suspended in blue,
close enough to touch, huge wings blanket the evening
and by virtue of tufted crest, yellow beak, blue throat,
we were immutably, precariously, nested.

How awkward a pair of amateurs we were,
fumbling in the grass, spilling wine and seed
while the stick-figure heron stood balanced on one leg,
listening for the inscrutable movement of tiny grubs,
the passionate positioning of the earth.

I hear the child's cry, your cry while bursting with milk.
The passage always swift, always unexpected and far
from the sweet, sticky, lactose world that tastes
of chalk, the heron hesitates, spreads its massive wings
and I am jealous of this ultimate succor.

In the cold late of lonely night, a bottle of scotch
and the game is solitaire played hard. The card's sharp slap
on the kitchen table like the beat of angry wings on an earth
continually shifting in ways that are unexpected, until night
finally recedes in the pale hope of dawn.

The endless series of green walls, slanted ceilings,
attic windows that did not vent the cigarette stained air.
The bumbling untrained hunter stumbles out the front door
and days become tiny dots on the horizon,
propelled by swift motion.

Of how the layers of chiffon unexpectedly swirled:
hair in high bouffant, a black dress, spaghetti straps,
lowest of décolletage, white shoulders, wide brown eyes
under bright chandeliers and our winged dreams of wild abandon,
always unexpected.

PETER KAROFF

To My Wife

Can it be true? Have we again
signed with our bodies' tenderest affinities
that enigmatic order blank? If you say
it's so, it must be so: you're always first,
quite naturally, to make sense of the words
the moon writes on your femininity.

And do you frown to read my wonder, my surprise,
as some complex anthology of awe
and diffidence, of pride and anguish,
jubilation and remorse? Gentle reader,
scanner of psychic skies, you've always seen
love's orbit's full of tears and always known
the tail of passion's comet is a shower of little cries;

nor can you miss the fact that all love's sighs
finally end in paradox, that what we buy
with life is death, that those with whom we joy
to be must always leave us or themselves be left:
and who can tell us what this girl or boy
will be: to us bereaver or by us bereft?

HALE CHATFIELD

A Pillowed Head

Matutinal. Mother-of-pearl
Summer come early. Slashed carmines
And washed milky blues.

To be first on the road,
Up with the ground mists and pheasants.
To be older and grateful

That this time you too were half-grateful
The pangs had begun. To be prepared
And clued in to the meaning

And trauma, and enter upon it
With full consent of the will.
(The first time, dismayed and arrayed

In your cut-off white cotton gown,
You were more bride than earth-mother
Up on the stirrup-rigged bed,

But now we were cool
To the point of a walk on the pier
Before you checked yourself in).

And then later on I half-fainted
When the little, slapped, palpable girl
Was handed to me; yet as usual

Came to in wide-open eyes
That had been farther dawned into
And wider, slower, duller

Than all those mornings of waiting
When your brow was a cairn of held silence
And the dawn chorus anything but.

SEAMUS HEANEY

A Locked House

As we drove back, crossing the hill,
The house still
Hidden in the trees, I always thought—
A fool's fear—that it might have caught
Fire, someone could have broken in.
As if things must have been
Too good here. Still, we always found
It locked tight, safe and sound.

I mentioned that, once, as a joke;
No doubt we spoke
Of the absurdity
To fear some dour god's jealousy
Of our good fortune. From the farm
Next door, our neighbors saw no harm
Came to the things we cared for here.
What did we have to fear?

Maybe I should have thought: all
Such things rot, fall—
Barns, houses, furniture.
We two are stronger than we were
Apart; we've grown
Together. Everything we own
Can burn; we know what counts—some such
Idea. We said as much.

We'd watched friends driven to betray;
Felt that love drained away
Some self they need.
We'd said love, like a growth, can feed
On hate we turn in and disguise;
We warned ourselves. That you might despise
Me—hate all we both loved best—
None of us ever guessed.

The house still stands, locked, as it stood
Untouched a good
Two years after you went.
Some things passed in the settlement;
Some things slipped away. Enough's left
That I come back sometimes. The theft
And vandalism were our own.
Maybe we should have known.

W. D. SNODGRASS

from *Woman*

And yet, how quickly the bride's veils evaporate!
A girl hesitates a moment in mid-air
And settles to the ground a wife, a mother.
Each evening a tired spirit visits
Her full house; wiping his feet upon a mat
Marked *Women and Children First,* the husband looks
At this grown woman. She stands there in slacks
Among the real world's appliances,
Women, and children; kisses him hello
Just as, that morning, she kissed him goodbye,
And he sits down, till dinner, with the paper.
This home of theirs is haunted by a girl's
Ghost. At sunset a woodpecker knocks
At a tree by the window, asking their opinion
Of life. The husband answers, "Life is life,"
And when his wife calls to him from the kitchen
He tells her who it was, and what he wanted.
Beating the whites of seven eggs, the beater
Asks her her own opinion; she says, "Life
Is life." "See how it sounds to say it isn't,"
The beater tempts her. "Life is not life,"
She says. It sounds the same. Putting her cake
Into the oven, she is satisfied
Or else dissatisfied: it sounds the same.
With knitted brows, with care's swift furrows nightly
Smoothed out with slow care, and come again with care
Each morning, she lives out her gracious life.

RANDALL JARRELL

Cutting the Jewish Bride's Hair

It's to possess more than the skin
that those old world Jews
exacted the hair of their brides.
    Good husband, lover of the Torah,
    does the calligraphy of your bride's hair
    interrupt your page?

Before the clownish friction of flesh
creating out of nothing
a mockup of its begetters,
a miraculous puppet of God,
you must first divorce her from her vanity.

She will snip off her pride,
cut back her appetite to be devoured,
she will keep herself well braided,
her love's furniture will not endanger you,
    but this little amputation
    will shift the balance of the universe.

RUTH WHITMAN

In Praise of Marriage

Marriage is a sweet state,
I can affirm it by my own experience,
In very truth, I who have a good and wise husband
Whom God helped me to find.
I give thanks to him who will save him for me,
For I can truly feel his great goodness
And for sure the sweet man loves me well.

Throughout that first night in our home,
I could well feel his great goodness,
For he did me no excess
That could hurt me.
But, before it was time to get up,
He kissed me 100 times, this I affirm,
Without exacting further outrage,
And yet for sure the sweet man loves me well.

He used to say to me in his soft language:
"God brought you to me,
Sweet lover, and I think he raised me
To be of use to you."
And then he did not cease to dream
All night, his conduct was so perfect,
Without seeking other excesses.
And yet for sure the sweet man loves me well.

O Princes, yet he drives me mad
When he tells me he is all mine;
He will destroy me with his gentle ways,
And yet for sure the sweet man loves me well.

CHRISTINE DE PISAN,
translation by C. Meredith Jones

Man and Wife

Tamed by *Miltown,* we lie on Mother's bed;
the rising sun in war paint dyes us red;
in broad daylight her gilded bed-posts shine,
abandoned, almost Dionysian.
At last the trees are green on Marlborough Street,
blossoms on our magnolia ignite
the morning with their murderous five days' white.
All night I've held your hand,
as if you had
a fourth time faced the kingdom of the mad—
its hackneyed speech, its homicidal eye—
and dragged me home alive. . . . Oh my *Petite,*
clearest of all God's creatures, still all air and nerve:
you were in your twenties, and I,
once hand on glass
and heart in mouth,
outdrank the Rahvs in the heat
of Greenwich Village, fainting at your feet—
too boiled and shy
and poker-faced to make a pass,
while the shrill verve
of your invective scorched the traditional South.

Now twelve years later, you turn your back.
Sleepless, you hold
your pillow to your hollows like a child;
your old-fashioned tirade—
loving, rapid, merciless—
breaks like the Atlantic Ocean on my head.

ROBERT LOWELL

Astronomical: A Marriage

He woke one morning, visionary,
like Copernicus, and told her his sun
no longer revolved around her continents,
that her moon could no longer sway his tides.

That Spring, she continued to water
the begonias, but failed to tie the stems
of the withered daffodils, which went
to seed, leaving an absence in the backyard
she would look at for years, but never rectify.

One night, he turned to her suggesting
that the world, after all, was perhaps flat,
but when they tried to sail off its edge
they always returned to the same house with its
empty rooms of furniture and photographs.

For years, they lived this way.
He took up ceramics. She ran in the Boston Marathon.
The magnolia continued to flower, but the wind
changed direction, and its fragrance was lost to them.
The neighborhood they lived in was rezoned: commercial.

She began to talk in her sleep, reciting
the names of planets and constellations, billowing
lines from poems he had read to her beneath the aspen.
She compared him to November and longed
for the barren sycamore. He compared her
to March and preferred the pasqueflower.

Winters, they walked along the ocean in search
of a shooting star. The surf pounded its temporary
quiet, phosphorescence sparkled on the white sands.
His hands shot, in recognition, towards the West—
"There," he whispered, "there."

"Where?" she answered, "where?"

Michael Blumenthal

The Husband and Wife Team

The two pianos of their past are a pair of ravens
Each with the shiny black wings of an iceberg.

Settled in the living room they melt

Infinitely slowly, little rivulets of tears trickle
Like sad lullabies down their sides . . .

Everywhere there's a dark throbbing.

Hollow, like the terrified breast
Of a seagull

Trapped, trying to get out

Even when they're silent
The sounding boards go right on protesting

But this is the center of the house, remember?

Dominating the concert hall
The giant portraits of our parents

Insist we go on playing for them

For each of us has a piano on his back
And sits in front of one forever.

With eyes like the polished depths
Of mahogany

The man looks at his wife over the black
Glistening humpback of a whale,

The woman sights along the lifted ridge
Of an open flying fish to see her husband

Full of overtones, the gold strings
Tangled like candy, like smooth satin

Valentines under the raised lids . . .

But even when they take bows together
At every anniversary accept, modestly

The applause they both deserve,

At night, in the bedroom
Each hears the other's quick breathing

(break)

Crouched behind gleaming muscles
And bright blood

They chew up the pages of the present
Greedily, separated from each other

By their own music

From a great distance they wave to each other
Riding their loud animals

Through caves of hammers descending

Each keeps his own time, together, with the upper
And lower halves of the keyboards their parents left them.

PATRICIA GOEDICKE

The Country Wife

She makes her way through the dark trees
Down to the lake to be alone.
Following their voices on the breeze,
She makes her way. Through the dark trees
The distant stars are all she sees.
They cannot light the way she's gone.
She makes her way through the dark trees
Down to the lake to be alone.

The night reflected on the lake,
The fire of stars changed into water.
She cannot see the winds that break
The night reflected on the lake
But knows they motion for her sake.
These are the choices they have brought her:
The night reflected on the lake,
The fire of stars changed into water.

DANA GIOIA

Foreign Affairs

We are two countries girded for the war,
Whisking our scouts across the pricked frontier
To ravage in each other's fields, cut lines
Along the lacework of strategic nerves,
Loot stores; while here and there,
In ambushes that trace a valley's curves,
Stark witness to the dangerous charge we bear,
A house ignites, a train's derailed, a bridge
Blows up sky-high, and water floods the mines.
Who first attacked? Who turned the other cheek?
Aggression perpetrated is as soon
Denied, and insult rubbed into the injury
By cunning agents trained in these affairs,
With whom it's touch-and-go, don't-tread-on-me,
I-dare-you-to, keep-off, and kiss-my-hand.
Tempers could sharpen knives, and do; we live
In states provocative
Where frowning headlines scare the coffee cream
And doomsday is the eighth day of the week.

Our exit through the slammed and final door
Is twenty times rehearsed, but when we face
The imminence of cataclysmic rupture,
A lesser pride goes down upon its knees.
Two countries separated by desire!—
Whose diplomats speed back and forth by plane,
Portmanteaus stuffed with fresh apologies
Outdated by events before they land.
Negotiations wear them out: they're driven mad
Between the protocols of tears and rapture.

Locked in our fated and contiguous selves,
These worlds that too much agitate each other,
Interdependencies from hip to head,
Twin principalities both slave and free,
We coexist, proclaiming Peace together,
Tell me no lies! We are divided nations
With malcontents by thousands in our streets,
These thousands torn by inbred revolutions.
A triumph is demanded, not moral victories
Deduced from small advances, small retreats.

Are the gods of our fathers not still daemonic?
On the steps of the Capitol
The outraged lion of our years roars panic,
And we suffer the guilty cowardice of the will,
Gathering its bankrupt slogans up for flight
Like gold from ruined treasuries.
And yet, and yet, although the murmur rises,
We are what we are, and only life surprises.

STANLEY KUNITZ

Some Nation Who's Been Slighted

Another country says she's breaking ties,
    calling back her diplomats, telling nationals
to pack. I know it's possible to have a change

    of heart, now or in the next century,
which is as close to us as a second hand
    to its mother 12. The other night I wanted to

push back from the table and never
    say another word to you, thinking it was what
you said I had to blame. I'm still learning

love only speaks to itself for so long,
    before it needs to hear what you have
to say. Whenever I feel like some nation

who's been slighted, this week like Britain,
    and want to break all ties, I think
of who died recently closest to me,

so I can say good-bye to her again and keep
    my suitcase in its closet, keep talking with you,
past midnight, in this our kitchen's embassy.

GARY MARGOLIS

Possession

The bulk, the heft
of our duties

to the physical
world. To the things

we call ours.
And our duties

to each other.
We get married,

and people ask,
What do you want?

Empty cartons
crowd the porch.

We buy each other
gifts and feel surrounded

by what we own,
what we thought

would comfort us.
You wake

from dreams
of other women, ready

to confess secrets,
your desire to tell

stronger than your desire
to protect me.

We move through
days of weather

the way we move
through our dreams:

not remembering
much but uneasy

(break)

afterwards anyway.
Tell me the truth,

we say to each other.
Is this what you wanted?

THERESA PAPPAS

VII

A Man and a Woman

But That Is Another Story

I do not think the ending can be right.
How can they marry and live happily
Forever, these who were so passionate
At chapter's end? Once they are settled in
The quiet country house, what will they do,
So many miles from anywhere?
Those blond Victorian ghosts crowding the stair,
Surely they disapprove? Ah me,
I fear love will catch cold and die
From pacing naked through those drafty halls
Night after night. Poor Frank! Poor Imogene!
Before them now their lives
Stretch empty as great Empire beds
After the lovers rise and the damp sheets
Are stripped by envious chambermaids.

And if the first night passes brightly enough,
What with the bonfires built of old love letters,
That is no inexhaustible fuel, I think.
A later dusk may find them, hand in hand,
Stopping among the folds to watch
The mating of the more ebullient sheep.
(And yet how soon the wool itself must lie
Scattered like snow, or miniature fallen clouds.)
God knows how it will end, not I.
Will Frank walk out one day
Alone through the ruined orchard with his stick,
Strewing the path with lissome heads
Of buttercups? Will Imogene
Conceal in the hollows of appointed oaks
Love notes for beardless gardeners and the like?

Meanwhile they quarrel, and make it up
Only to quarrel again. A sudden storm
Pulls the last fences down. The stupid sheep
Stand out all night now coughing in the garden
And peering through the windows where they sleep.

DONALD JUSTICE

Days We Would Rather Know

There are days we would rather know
than these, as there is always, later,
a wife we would rather have married
than whom we did, in that severe nowness
time pushed, imperfectly, to then. Whether,
standing in the museum before Rembrandt's "Juno,"
we stand before beauty, or only before a consensus
about beauty, is a question that makes all beauty
suspect . . . and all marriages. Last night,
leaves circled the base of the gingko as if
the sun had shattered during the night
into a million gold coins no one had the sense
to claim. And now, there are days we would
rather know than these, days when to stand
before beauty and before "Juno" are, convincingly,
the same, days when the shattered sunlight
seeps through the trees and the women we marry
stay interesting and beautiful both at once,
and their men. And though there are days
we would rather know than now, I am,
at heart, a scared and simple man. So I tighten
my arms around the woman I love, now
and imperfectly, stand before "Juno" whispering
beautiful beautiful until I believe it, and—
when I come home at night—I run out
into the day's pale dusk with my broom
and my dustpan, sweeping the coins from the base
of the ginkgo, something to keep for a better tomorrow:
days we would rather know that never come.

MICHAEL BLUMENTHAL

Letter Home

FOR L.

Last night during a thunderstorm,
awakened and half-awake,
I wanted to climb into bed
on my mother's side, be told
everything's all right—
the mother-lie which gives us power
to make it true.
Then I realized she was dead,
that you're the one I sleep with
and rely on, and I wanted you.
The thunder brought what thunder brings.
I lay there, trembling,
thinking what perfect sense we make
of each other when we're afraid
or half-asleep or alone.

Later the sky was all stars,
the obvious ones and those
you need to look at a little sideways
until they offer themselves.
I wanted to see them all—
wanted too much, you'd say—
like this desire to float
between the egg and the grave,
unaccountable, neither lost nor found,
then wanting the comfortable
orthodoxies of home.

I grew up thinking home was a place
you left with a bat
in your hands; you came back dirty
or something was wrong.
Only bad girls were allowed
to roam as often or as far.
Shall we admit
that because of our bodies
your story can never be mine,
mine never yours?
That where and when they intersect
is the greatest intimacy we'll ever have?

(break)

Every minute or so a mockingbird
delivers its repertoire.
Here's my blood
in the gray remains of a mosquito.
I know I'm just another slug
in the yard, but that's not what
my body knows.
The boy must die is the lesson
hardest learned.
I'll be home soon. Will you understand
if not forgive
that I expect to be loved
beyond deserving, as always?

      Saratoga, 1984

                             STEPHEN DUNN

Liebesgedicht

I love you as my other self, as the other
self of the tree is not the pale tree
in the flat hand of the river, but the earth
that holds, is held by, the root of the tree.
This is how the earth loves the river,
and why its least fold solicits each
impulsive stream until the gathered water
makes of earth a passage to the sea.

I'd like to draw a lesson from this figure,
and find some comfort in the way the larger
world rings with such dependencies.
But if I see ourselves in earth and water,
I also see one taken from the other,
the rivening wind loosed against the tree.

ELLEN BRYANT VOIGHT

The Marriage Nocturne

Stopped at a corner, near midnight, I watch
A young man and young woman quarreling
Under the streetlamp. What I can see is gestures.
He leans forward, he scowls, raises his hand.
She has been taking it, but now she stands
Up to him, throwing her chin and chest out.
The stoplight purples their two leather jackets.
Both of them now are shouting, theatrical,
Shut up, bitch, or, Go to hell, loser,
And between them, in a stroller,
Sits their pale bundled baby, a piece of candy.

Earlier this evening I was listening
To the poet Amichai, whose language seemed
To grow like Jonah's gourd in a dry place,
From pure humility, or perhaps from yearning
For another world, land, city
Of Jerusalem, while embracing this one,
As a man dreams of the never-obtainable mistress,
Flowery, perfumed, girlish
(But hasn't she somehow been promised to him?)
And meanwhile has and holds the stony wife
Whom the Lord gives him for a reproach.

I can imagine, when such a husband touches
Such a wife, hating it, in tears,
And helpless lust, and the survivor's shame,
That her eyes gaze back at him like walls
Where you still can see the marks of the shelling.

We make beauty of bitterness. Woman and man,
Arab and Jew, we have arrived at that
Dubious skill. Still, when one of these children,
Having moved like a dancer, smashes the other
One in the face, and the baby swivels its periscope
Neck to look, I will not see it:
The light changes. Fifteen miles down the road,
That will be lined by luminous spring trees,
My husband reads in bed, sleepy and naked;
I am not crying, I step on the gas, I am driving
Home to my marriage, my safety, through this wounded
World that we cannot heal, that is our bride.

ALICIA OSTRIKER

A Man and a Woman

Between a man and a woman
The anger is greater, for each man would like to sleep
In the arms of each woman who would like to sleep
In the arms of each man, if she trusted him not to be
Schizophrenic, if he trusted her not to be
A hypochondriac, if she trusted him not to leave her
Too soon, if he trusted her not to hold him
Too long, and often women stare at the word men
As it lives in the word women, as if each woman
Carried a man inside her and a woe, and has
Crying fits that last for days, not like the crying
Of a man, which lasts a few seconds, and rips the throat
Like a claw—but because the pain differs
Much as the shape of the body, the woman takes
The suffering of the man for selfishness, the man
The woman's pain for helplessness, the woman's lack of it
For hardness, the man's tenderness for deception,
The woman's lack of acceptance, an act of contempt
Which is really fear, the man's fear for fickleness,
Yet cars come off the bridge in rivers of light
Each holding a man and a woman.

ALAN FELDMAN

Marriage

The arrangement is essentially comic,
silent, and familiar to the audience:
you walk, and then I, six feet behind.
We are carrying something between us,
not visible, but obvious enough.

We are careful, though not beyond reason;
we do this every day. The audience
knows what to expect: the hero comes,
intent on his labors, of which we have
no part. Whatever he is doing,
we are only here to make things difficult;
that is, to go on doing what we are doing,
being careful, but not beyond reason.

You pass; always the gentleman, he waits.
Between you and me the distance is endless;
the audience catches its breath. Now.
Flattened against the glass his handsome
empty face registers the first flicker of surprise.

I pass. He will continue his labors;
he will return, presently, bearing
for the heroine a cluster of wilted flowers.
We go on. The audience no longer notices
that we continue to bear between us
something invisible, difficult to manage,
fragile, and slightly besmeared.

DONALD FINKEL

After the Argument

Whoever spoke first would lose something,
    that was the stupid
        unspoken rule.

The stillness would be a clamor, a capo
    on a nerve. He'd stare
        out the window,

she'd put away dishes, anything
    for some noise. They'd sleep
        in different rooms.

The trick was to speak as if you hadn't
    spoken, a comment
        so incidental

it wouldn't be counted as speech.
    Or to touch while passing,
        an accident

of clothing, billowy sleeve against
    rolled-up cuff. They couldn't
        stand hating

each other for more than one day.
    Each knew this, each knew
        the other's body

would begin to lean, the voice yearn
    for the familiar confluence
        of breath and syllable.

When? Who first? It was Yalta, always
    on some level the future,
        the next time.

                    This time

there was a cardinal on the bird feeder;
    one of them was shameless enough
        to say so, the other pleased

to agree. And their sex was a knot
    untying itself, a prolonged
        coming loose.

STEPHEN DUNN

Thrust & Parry

You're sure you heard something break. Something snap.
Deep within her. Like a twig split in two
And cast in the fire. Or like the snap
Of a violin string, halting all music.
And witnessing tears break in her face
You discovered the magic, the black magic,
Of your words, no magic could take back.
And, loathing the terrifying maniac in you,
You shattered a vase of flowers and fled,
As if from yourself, out into the dark.
Leaving her to pick up the flowers,
Restring the violin, await your next attack,
But this time of fawning words & flowers,
And her breakfast in bed for at least a week.

GREG DELANTY

At the Funeral of the Marriage

At the funeral of the marriage
My wife and I paced
On either side of the hearse,
Our children racing behind it . . .
As the coffin was emptied
Down into the bottomless grave,
Our children stood in a half-circle,
Playing on flutes and recorders.
My wife and I held hands.
While the mourners wept and the gravediggers
Unfurled shovelfuls of clay
Down on top of the coffin,
We slowly walked away,
Accomplices beneath the yew trees.
We had a cup of tea in the graveyard café
Across the street from the gates:
We discussed the texture of the undertaker's face,
Its beetroot quality.
As I gazed at my wife
I wondered who on earth she was—
I saw that she was a green-eyed stranger.
I said to her: Would you like to go to a film?
She said: I would love to go to a film.
In the back seats of the cinema,
As we slid up and down in our seats
In a frenzy of hooks and clasps,
The manager courteously asked us not to take off our clothes.
We walked off urgently through the rain-strewn streets
Into a leaf-sodden cul-de-sac
And as, from the tropic isle of our bed,
Chock-a-block with sighs & cries,
We threw our funeral garments on the floor,
We could hear laughter outside the door.
There is no noise children love more to hear
Than the noise of their parents making love:
O my darling, who on earth are you?

PAUL DURCAN

VIII

The Ache of Marriage

The Ache of Marriage

The ache of marriage:

thigh and tongue, beloved,
are heavy with it,
it throbs in the teeth

We look for communion
and are turned away, beloved,
each and each

It is leviathan and we
in its belly
looking for joy, some joy
not to be known outside it

two by two in the ark of
the ache of it.

DENISE LEVERTOV

For My Husband

Is it a dream,
the way we huddle over the board,
our fingers touching on the slick button?
The Ouija stammers under so much doubt,
finally reaches L, then O,
pauses under its lettered heaven,
and as it veers toward *loss* and the long past
that lodges with us, you press toward *love,*
and the disk stalls
                outside
a cry is loosed from the bay,
but you are looking for two swans
on a glass lake, a decade of roses—
oh my lonely, my precious loaf,
can't we say outloud the parent word,
longing,
        whose sad head
looms over any choice you make?

ELLEN BRYANT VOIGHT

Drift

Lying in bed this morning
you read to me of continental drift,
how Africa and South America
sleeping once side by side
slowly slid apart;
how California even now
pushes off like a swimmer
from the country's edge, along
the San Andreas Fault.
And I thought about you and me
who move in sleep each night
to the far reaches of the bed,
ranges of blankets between us.
It is a natural law this drift
and though we break it
as we break bread
over and over again, you remain
Africa with your deep shade,
your heat. And I, like California,
push off from your side
my two feet cold
against your back, dreaming
of Asia Minor.

LINDA PASTAN

Outlook Uncertain

No season
brings conclusion.

Each year,
through heartache, nightmare,

true loves alter,
marriages falter,

and lovers illumine
the antique design,

apart, together,
foolish as weather,

right as rain,
sure as ruin.

Must you, then, and I
adjust the whole sky

over every morning;
or else, submitting

to cloud and storm,
enact the same

lugubrious ending,
new lives pending?

ALASTAIR REID

Quarrel

Since morning they have been quarreling—
the sun pouring its implacable white bath
over the birches, each one undressing
slyly, from the top down—and they hammer
at each other with their knives, nailfiles,
graters of complaint as the day unwinds,
the plush clouds lowering a gray matte
for the red barn. Lunch, the soup
like batting in their mouths, last week,
last year, they're moving on to always
and never, their shrill pitiful children
crowd around but they see the top of this
particular mountain, its glacial headwall,
the pitch is terrific all through dinner,
and they are committed, the sun long gone,
the two of them back to back in the blank
constricting bed, like marbles on aluminum—
O this fierce love
that needs to reproduce in one another
wounds inflicted by the world.

ELLEN BRYANT VOIGHT

Patience

Since you're the woman I love,
why do I keep looking? as if
another could satisfy some need
you are blind to, as if her hand
might touch wounds that won't heal
in your presence.

She was the one I dared wait for:
late-night dream-walker, sister
and missing bone, dark mirror.
Blonde when I wanted blonde, wet
when my hand reached her, yes
to all my questions.

Yet I couldn't rise to her
expectations—I wasn't that gifted
in darkness, after all. I was no
wizard, no sorcerer. I loved
her body the way you might love
roses or a fine Victorian inkwell.

I wanted to dip myself into her
again and again, to write
the missing chapters of my life
in her body. But I couldn't
take her into my mind the way
you take me into your arms:

Wholly. Recklessly. Yielding
all pretense. With her
I was naked but guarded: she
was a drug. Amoral. Un-
predictable. Inconstant.

She was a vision, and you
a splinter that nests in my heart.
You wound me, and I can't stop
taking you in. This is a blood
contract between us.

(break)

You are writing something inside
me with your sharp tongue,
with your loyal blood, with your
infinite patience. Some day,
your true faith tells you,
I will read what is etched there:

Rest, lover, you have no more to prove.

CHARLES FISHMAN

Just Married

In the hammock, still white as a bridal gown,
the Father's Day gift, you feel the sun
fall through the first lacy outcroppings
of maple leaves, a hot green light
on your eyelids, and it's the same
easy floating you found her in that day
you woke inside her breath, pine sifting
audibly, the mockingbird playing his chords
over and over as if he knew you'd forget.

A life later, kids in school, no work today,
the bird sings, bringing back the service
performed by the justice of the peace, two
witnesses plucked from the sidewalk, and
now the little cries she made stir inside
your head where that green shadow drifts.
Awake, you slipped to the cottage window,
not wanting to be cruel, left her sleeping,
tugged on pants, strolled barefoot, hummed.

The pine cones hurt, but the river was cool
enough, so you walked, found the farmer
burying the spotted foal, sweat in his eyes.
Hunched on his fence you named your love
until he was done, until he spat and told
the story of the local doctor who never saw
a thing as the husband's knife slipped in
across the balls he was pumping with. Brown
teeth in the farmer's mouth gleamed then.
Your heart skittered like a small animal's.

Whatever love is, it is not a bird's song
you think as you feel the gray fingers
of clouds turn above you. Now you look up
where the mockingbird rasps on, ordinary
as the new moan of the hammock that means
only weight, change, the body that bends
around you, but not as she did, as light.
Now there's the sweat in the small cradle
of your back, the cruelty of crying out
the way you burst back on her, not caring
if anyone was with her, murderous, blank.

DAVE SMITH

Trouble in the Portable Marriage

"What whiteness will you add to this whiteness, what candor?"

We walk the dirt road toward town through the clear evening.
The sky is apricot behind the black cane. Pink above,
and dull raspberry on the Turkish hills across the water.
The Aegean is light by the shore, then dark farther out.
I cannot distinguish now which is light and which is color.
I go up the road on my bicycle, floating in the air:
the moon enlarging and decreasing moving all the time
close to my head. I stop at the bridge.
Get off and sit on the rail because I remember
I have no money. After a while you come.
Your hand touches me and then withdraws.
We talk about why the moon changes size, and I think
how I'd smelled it. Like sweet leaf smoke,
like sweet wood burning. We go toward town together,
me riding and you walking. Feeling the silk and paleness
of the air. No one passes us the whole length of the road.

LINDA GREGG

Leaving

At dusk they watched the glassy lake,
the fragile family of wooden boats,

the sky which dreamily shifted its palette
so she wanted to fix a violet moment

of light to keep, a place she'd come
back to alone, wherever she stayed.

When they turned away, tiny
figures fishing for trout disappeared.

Only a year, he said, after
so many inviolate years.

But what if it weren't a year, what
happens when one of them leaves

forever? That night, they lay in the secretive
air, dazed by departure's cycles

of deaths and rebirths. Now when she thinks
of him, she sees the grave lake

behind him, three islands adrift,
beyond reach. At dawn, it was herself

she heard in the slow, scared
throb of the mourning dove's song.

GAIL MAZUR

Horse

What does the horse give you
that I cannot give you?

I watch you when you are alone,
when you ride into the field behind the dairy,
your hands buried in the mare's
dark mane.

Then I know what lies behind your silence:
scorn, hatred of me, of marriage. Still,
you want me to touch you; you cry out
as brides cry, but when I look at you I see
there are no children in your body.
Then what is there?

Nothing, I think. Only haste
to die before I die.

In a dream, I watched you ride the horse
over the dry fields and then
dismount: you two walked together;
in the dark, you had no shadows.
But I felt them coming toward me
since at night they go anywhere,
they are their own masters.

Look at me. You think I don't understand?
What is the animal
if not passage out of this life?

LOUISE GLÜCK

Adam and Eve in Later Life

On getting out of bed the one says, "Ouch!"
The other "What?" and when the one says "I said
'Ouch,' " the other says, "All right, you needn't shout."

Deucalion and Pyrrha, Darby and Joan, Philemon and Baucis,
Tracy and Hepburn—if this can happen to Hepburn
No one is safe—all rolled up into two,
Contented with the cottage and the cottage cheese
And envied only by ambitious gods . . .

Later, over coffee, they compare the backs of their hands
And conclude they are slowly being turned into lizards.
But nothing much surprises them these days.

HOWARD NEMEROV

The Figures on the Frieze

Darkness wears off and, dawning into daylight,
they find themselves unmagically together.
He sees the stains of morning in her face.
She shivers, distant in his bitter weather.

Diminishing of legend sets him brooding.
Great goddess-figures conjured from his book
blur what he sees with bafflement of wishing.
Sulky, she feels his fierce, accusing look.

Familiar as her own, his body's landscape
seems harsh and dull to her habitual eyes.
Mystery leaves and, mercilessly flying,
The blind fiends come, emboldened by her cries.

Avoiding simple reach of hand for hand
(which would surrender pride), by noon they stand
withdrawn from touch, reproachfully alone,
small in each other's eyes, tall in their own.

Wild with their misery, they entangle now
in baffling agonies of why and how.
Afternoon glimmers, and they wound anew,
flesh, nerve, bone, gristle in each other's view.

'What have you done to me?' From each proud heart,
new phantoms loom in the deceiving air.
As the light fails, each is consumed apart,
he by his ogre vision, she by her fire.

When night falls, out of a despair of daylight,
they strike the lying attitudes of love,
and through the perturbations of their bodies,
each feels the amazing, murderous legends move.

ALASTAIR REID

From the Night-Window

The night rattles with nightmares.
Children cry in the close-packed houses,
A man rots in his snoring.
On quiet feet, policemen test doors.
Footsteps become people under streetlamps.
Drunks return from parties,
Sounding of empty bottles and old songs.
The young women come home,
The pleasure in them deafens me.
They trot like small horses
And disappear into white beds
At the edge of the night.
All windows open, this hot night.
And the sleepless, smoking in the dark,
Making small red lights at their mouths,
Count the years of their marriages.

DOUGLAS DUNN

Equinox 1980

In the stillness after dawn we two
    paddled a noiseless boat
before wakefall across
    a bay smooth as a mirror,
changeless as its glass.
    Not a whisper of passage.
Hardly a single stir
    inside the horizon
except for the rippling
    wrinkles pushed by our prow
and the faraway swoop and flurry
    of a squadron of terns.
The tide at its landward edge
    ignited a smudge of
    commotion,
skittering sandpipers
    along the farther shore.
In all the days of our marriage
    we had never seen
so unruffled a morning:
    never had any event
shimmered with so costly a light
    as we ascended the meandering
creek in our sweet boat,
    surprising no one except
a bright-eyed otter.
    Pushed by mere hints
from our paddles,
    we rode up the thickening tide
among heavy wands
    of ripe marsh grass
that wagged seed-bundles
    high above our heads.

(break)

Neither one speaking,
　　　 we rose to go ashore
and lugged away
　　　 our featherweight kayak
to winter quarters,
　　　 knowing as we stowed it
that this would be the last time,
　　　 that we would never set out to sea
together again.

PETER DAVISON

IX

From Grief to Grief

Love crosses its islands, from grief to grief

Love crosses its islands, from grief to grief,
it sets its roots, watered with tears,
and no one—no one—can escape the heart's progress
as it runs, silent and carnivorous.

You and I searched for a wide valley, for another planet
where the salt wouldn't touch your hair,
where sorrows couldn't grow because of anything I did,
where bread could live and not grow old.

A planet entwined with vistas and foliage,
a plain, a rock, hard and unoccupied:
we wanted to build a strong nest

with our own hands, without hurt or harm or speech,
but love was not like that: love was a lunatic city
with crowds of people blanching on their porches.

PABLO NERUDA
translated by Stephen Tapscott

Separated

The day slants
toward the light it is about to become
and, deep from your borrowed bed,
you rise, alone again
as in your happiest hours,
and you wonder, as you ease yourself
toward the lit corner of the room
where dawn first claims the house,
why, and for what, a man or woman
would barter these first, uninhabited hours
in which the mind moves
like a freshly lit candle
from the near-death of sleep
into the first, warm syllables
of its own creation, in which time moves
like a concertina through its three-tiered scales
and the day becomes, as it should be,
the slow unwinding of the self's discourse
with the self. Fresh from your solipsistic sleep,
you are what you are again: the slim feather
of your own life, a swelled paragraph
in your own book, and you wonder why
a vague guilt drifts into the unshared hours,
why the relinquished bliss passes,
in the secular world, for a kind of nobility,
because today, above all else, you feel
noble once more, like a priest too long banished
from his church, like an exiled king
returning to his kingdom, and you ponder,
in the baptismal light, what guilt,
what sense of unentitlement to your own plenitude,
had brought you there, into the divisive symmetry
of the conjugal bed, and you repeat to yourself
what you have always known courage to be—
the hard resilience to say: *I did, I was,*
I said, I am, the claimed and peculiar light
of your own strange shining. Risen perfectly now
into the shape of your hard-won selfhood,
you sit at the window watching the bricks
become the building and the leaves the trees,

the day relinquish itself to the human world,
which you, praise God, feel part of
once more—but never again too much,
never again like that.

MICHAEL BLUMENTHAL

After the Division

There it is: In an unbleached photograph,
Plato's two halves of man-and-woman, cast
of our shadows, sliced and joined again: four arms,
four legs, two heads. Metallic, silver-gray,

that blade clicks from our feet at acute angles
from our bodies, then it becomes a gaunt,
barbarous giant and creeps toward the sea.
Below us, in the foreground, the white sand

is ruffled now by footsole indentations,
and you, above the tracks, a leggy matador,
brandish a towel the sun has gored blood red.
You search the land; musing behind your shoulder,

I watch the ocean. After that sun fell,
we cracked apart. I listened for your silences
in clamorous voices; looked for your merest
accidental glance among the customary

diurnal predators. With quartz-clear eyes,
you'd tell me I looked lovely in a torn
dress, but question natural laws. Remember
the night you challenged probability,

tossing a coin to count one hundred heads
until the dawn, an enterprise that lulled
me, but held you fast. You would not ponder
gravity, compelled instead by bonds

between revolving worlds and fallen apples.
Driven by what anemones are made of,
not by their names, calm, you would insist
that viruses have viruses, and cells

have dictionaries, and even memories.
With quiet fortitude and dour tenacity,
probing a cloud, examining a dahlia,
godless, you'd lead me to my God. One day,

in solitude, I caught your stalky form
jack-knifed over a lean golden retriever,
and avenues spun like planets. There was time.
One night I watched El Greco's Cardinal

(break)

sprout your weedy beard. Still, there was time.
Unlike Dante's damned, who see the future,
but not the past, I reel in what there was,
and wish when we had marched on brittle leaves

to *L'Internationale,* that shadows drawn
into our forms at noon, were visible.
Tonight we walk under the same mimosa trees
and wonder why we severed then; creepers

hooked into oaks to live, we held too fast,
when earth and sun—all things, irregular—
converge and separate. We ask again
why we merged to want this moment now,

and see only the creature in the photograph
(though whether it has life, as you would say,
is philosophical, depending on
degrees of selfhood), but, in any case,

a being, torn in two, grown whole, the root
our bodies spring from, moves discreetly
toward the sea. After twelve years apart,
I watch its steely edges cut the sand,

and know it will glide, unseen, even when day
concludes. I wake with you and feel the sun
invent one shadow that starts out from us,
and know the time has come to begin our lives.

GRACE SCHULMAN

Good-bye. Sweet Dreams. Come Back.

A porchlight flared over the lawn,
And you were just in love, leaving,
Your whole body bronze.

You had planned to go on
Counting houses down the block,
Cross over at the frosted lamp,

And then look back.
As she should have been, she was,

Forward on the porch,
Waving good-bye, yours.

All you could think of then
Was growing old beautifully together.
Down the years,

A lane of oaks first- and second-growth,
Sparrows that had been
Chattering and boxing in the leaves

Long since settled into grass and fluff.

In her cold, in her yellow cotton dress,
She couldn't stay, and was gone

By the time you stopped and
Turned to see her, as she should have been,
Dark and forward, back-lit, waving.

ARTHUR SMITH

Man and Wife

You were a unit when I saw you last:
The handsome husband and the happy wife,
Which was an act; but tissue of the past
Between you, unseen, made you one for life,

Or so I thought. It seems that I was wrong.
Seeing you ten years later, the kids grown
And gone, the still light of the long
Living room coming between you, I should have known

The lines were down. Your life went on with such
Attention to unchange: each "darling" fell
With metered carelessness; each "please" with much
Conviction; each "thanks" rang true as a bell.

But when you walked me to the door to go,
I saw the fault between your faces. Oh.

L. E. SISSMAN

The Marriage

Under its angry skin, her grief
ripens: succulent, wound-color.
She knew there were other women—
his baroque excuses for silence—
but knew in the weaker hemisphere
of her heart, that stringent
muscle pumping in, valved open.
Hinged clam, living for fifteen years
on grit and gravel, housed now against
the weather, she has the car, the kids,
an appetite for garbage. He's got
a new wife, wants her to take him in,
produce a pearl.

ELLEN BRYANT VOIGHT

Here Are My Black Clothes

I think now it is better to love no one
than to love you. Here are my black clothes,
the tired nightgowns and robes fraying
in many places. Why should they hang useless
as though I were going naked? You liked me well enough
in black; I make you a gift of these objects.
You will want to touch them with your mouth, run
your fingers through the thin
tender underthings and I
will not need them in my new life.

LOUISE GLÜCK

No More Marriages

Well, there ain't going to be no more marriages.
And no goddam honeymoons. Not if I can help it.
Not that I don't like men,
being in bed with them and all. It's the rest.
And that's what happens, isn't it? All those people
that get littler together. I want things
to happen to me the proper size.
The moon and the salmon and me and the fir trees
they're all the same size and they live together.
I'm the worse part, but mean no harm.
I might scare a deer, but I walk and breathe
as quiet as a person can learn.
If I'm not like my grandmother's garden
that smelled sweet all over and was warm
as a river, I do go up the mountain
to see the birds close and look
at the moon just come visible and lie down
to look at it with my face open.
Guilty or not, though, there won't be no post
cards made up of my life with Delphi on them.
Not even if I have to eat alone all those years.
They're never going to do that to me.

LINDA GREGG

River Road

That year of the cloud, when my marriage failed,
I slept in a chair, by the flagstone hearth,
fighting my sleep,
and one night saw a Hessian soldier
stand at attention there in full
regalia, till his head broke into flames.
My only other callers were the FBI
sent to investigate me as a Russian spy
by patriotic neighbors on the river road;
and flying squirrels parachuting from the elms
who squeaked in rodent heat between the walls
and upstairs rumbled at their nutty games.
I never dared open the attic door.
Even my nervous Leghorns joined the act,
indulging their taste for chicken from behind.
A glazed look swam into the survivors' eyes;
they caught a sort of dancing-sickness,
a variation of the blind staggers,
that hunched their narrow backs, and struck
a stiffened wing akimbo,
as round and round the poultry yard
they flapped and dropped and flapped again.
The county agent shook his head:
not one of them was spared the cyanide.

That year of the cloud, when my marriage failed,
I paced up and down the bottom-fields,
tamping the mud-puddled nurslings in
with a sharp blow of the heel
timed to the chop-chop of the hoe:
red pine and white, larch, balsam fir,
one stride apart, two hundred to the row,
until I heard from Rossiter's woods
the downward spiral of a veery's song
unwinding on the eve of war.

(break)

Lord! Lord! who has lived so long?
Count it ten thousand trees ago,
five houses and ten thousand trees,
since the swallows exploded from Bowman Tower
over the place where the hermit sang,
while I held a fantail of squirming roots
that kissed the palm of my dirty hand,
as if in reply to a bird.
The stranger who hammers No Trespass signs
to the staghorn sumac along the road
must think he owns this property.
I park my car below the curve
and climbing over the tumbled stones
where the wild foxgrape perseveres,
I walk into the woods I made,
my dark and resinous, blistered land,
through the deep litter of the years.

STANLEY KUNITZ

Winter Remembered

Two evils, monstrous either one apart,
Possessed me, and were long and loath at going:
A cry of Absence, Absence, in the heart,
And in the wood the furious winter blowing.

Think not, when fire was bright upon my bricks,
And past the tight boards hardly a wind could enter,
I glowed like them, the simple burning sticks,
Far from my cause, my proper heat and center.

Better to walk forth in the frozen air
And wash my wound in the snows; that would be healing;
Because my heart would throb less painful there,
Being caked with cold, and past the smart of feeling.

And where I walked, the murderous winter blast
Would have this body bowed, these eyeballs streaming,
And though I think this heart's blood froze not fast
It ran too small to spare one drop for dreaming.

Dear love, these fingers that had known your touch,
And tied our separate forces first together,
Were ten poor idiot fingers not worth much,
Ten frozen parsnips hanging in the weather.

JOHN CROWE RANSOM

Divorce

I have killed our lives together,
axed off each head,
with their poor blue eyes stuck in a beach ball
rolling separately down the drive.
I have killed all the good things,
but they are too stubborn for me.
They hang on.
The little words of companionship
have crawled into their graves,
the thread of compassion,
dear as a strawberry,
the mingling of bodies
that bore two daughters within us,
the look of you dressing,
early,
all the separate clothes, neat and folded,
you sitting on the edge of the bed
polishing your shoes with boot black,
and I loved you then, so wise from the shower,
and I loved you many other times
and I have been, for months,
trying to drown it,
to push it under,
to keep its great red tongue
under like a fish,
but wherever I look they are on fire,
the bass, the bluefish, the wall-eyed flounder
blazing among the kelp and seaweed
like many suns battering up the waves
and my love stays bitterly glowing,
spasms of it will not sleep,
and I am helpless and thirsty and need shade
but there is no one to cover me—
not even God.

ANNE SEXTON

Hymn to a Broken Marriage

Dear Nessa—Now that our marriage is over
I would like you to know that, if I could put back the clock
Fifteen years to the cold March day of our wedding,
I would wed you again and, if that marriage also broke,
I would wed you yet again and, if it a third time broke,
Wed you again, and again, and again, and again, and again:
If you would have me which, of course, you would not
For, even you—in spite of your patience and your innocence
(Strange characteristics in an age such as our own)—
Even you require to shake off the addiction of romantic love
And seek, instead, the herbal remedy of a sane affection
In which are mixed in profuse and fair proportion
Loverliness, brotherliness, fatherliness:
A sane man could not espouse a more intimate friend than you.

PAUL DURCAN

Wedding-Ring

My wedding-ring lies in a basket
as if at the bottom of a well.
Nothing will come to fish it back up
and onto my finger again.
                                    It lies
among keys to abandoned houses,
nails waiting to be needed and hammered
into some wall,
telephone numbers with no names attached,
idle paperclips.
                        It can't be given away
for fear of bringing ill-luck.
                                    It can't be sold
for the marriage was good in its own
time, though that time is gone.
                                    Could some artificer
beat into it bright stones, transform it
into a dazzling circlet no one could take
for solemn betrothal or to make promises
living will not let them keep? Change it
into a simple gift I could give in friendship?

DENISE LEVERTOV

The Marriage

The wind comes from opposite poles,
traveling slowly.

She turns in the deep air.
He walks in the clouds.

She readies herself,
shakes out her hair,

makes up her eyes,
smiles.

The sun warms her teeth,
the tip of her tongue moistens them.

He brushes the dust from his suit
and straightens his tie.

He smokes.
Soon they will meet.

The wind carries them closer.
They wave.

Closer, closer.
They embrace.

She is making a bed.
He is pulling off his pants.

They marry
and have a child.

The wind carries them off
in different directions.

The wind is strong, he thinks
as he straightens his tie.

I like this wind, she says
as she puts on her dress.

The wind unfolds.
The wind is everything to them.

MARK STRAND

X

Love Recognized

from *Idea*

Since there's no help, come, let us kiss and part!
Nay, I have done, you get no more of me;
And I am glad, yea, glad with all my heart,
That thus so cleanly I myself can free.
Shake hands for ever, cancel all our vows;
And when we meet at any time again,
Be it not seen in either of our brows,
That we one jot of former love retain.
Now at the last gasp of Love's latest breath,
When, his pulse failing, Passion speechless lies,
When Faith is kneeling by his bed of death,
And Innocence is closing up his eyes,—
Now, if thou wouldst, when all have given him over,
From death to life thou might'st him yet recover.

MICHAEL DRAYTON

Revisions

Make it new . . .
EZRA POUND

It's a bit like working
on a marriage that has gone
wrong somewhere, but not quite
wrong enough to abandon—

Each morning,
the fact of the marriage
faces you like your
no-longer-perfect skin
in the mirror:

It merely IS,
something you have uttered
that all the inhalations
in the world will not
make clean again.

You hold it to the light,
try to remember the faith
you felt when you first agreed
to make its life your own.

You ask yourself to believe
what held you then, though it
was the stars, and tonight
there ARE no stars.

Your poem looks at you, like Pound,
and says *let's make it new, baby,
let's start the whole damn thing
over again.* You smile at her

Good intentions, erase another
superfluous comma, a redundant
adjective, delete another line-
break that makes your breath
come short when you kiss her.

(break)

You put your arm around her,
though she's not nearly as beautiful
as she was then, not nearly as perfect
as you had hoped. You try

To console her, you tell her *nothing*
can make your marriage new again—

Only better, love,
only better.

MICHAEL BLUMENTHAL

Ars Poetica

Think of it, nine thousand
breakfasts together, and now
coffee again for the first time: what
a virginal movement it is, this
silvering together, every day
the very first day, every night
the first night, not a film replayed, more
like pages in a long book, strata
in these limestone hills we live in,
two billion years old.
We're not yet as old as the limestone,
but we're catching up—or rather,
reducing the proportion, like a kid brother
gaining on his elders; we're gaining
on the limestone and
beginning to see
it's an art, like Cellini's, this
silvering—like poetry, reminding us
in its earnest, nagging way,
that every new minute we risk
immortality, surviving
for nine thousand days by luck or cunning;
but at the end we're sent to press
with all our typos intact, fossils, captive
in the ancient rock. Meanwhile,
we're all such fumblers, gauche,
all thumbs: maybe
poems and marriages deal
mostly in failures—on the way to shape,
nine thousand blemishes hitching a ride. Maybe
only a poem or a silver bowl
will tell us as well as love: that
these are the only raw
materials we have—the painful
moments of wonder,
the small, well-meant betrayals, rain
in the limestone hills.
Well, we're not finished yet;
the revisions are still in process, a line here,
a day there, the whole thing

taking on a kind of polished
mutilation, a scarred silver florin,
a weathered hill,
an epic fragment.
There's time yet to get it—not right,
of course, but anyway revised,
emended, more mature
in its lumpy way. Think of it,
two billion years of shaping:
it's a beginning.

PHILIP APPLEMAN

For What Binds Us

There are names for what binds us:
strong forces, weak forces.
Look around, you can see them:
the skin that forms in a half-empty cup,
nails rusting into the places they join,
joints dovetailed on their own weight.
The way things stay so solidly
wherever they've been set down—
and gravity, scientists say, is weak.

And see how the flesh grows back
across a wound, with a great vehemence,
more strong
than the simple, untested surface before.
There's a name for it on horses,
when it comes back darker and raised: proud flesh,

as all flesh
is proud of its wounds, wears them
as honors given out after battle,
small triumphs pinned to the chest—

And when two people have loved each other
see how it is like a
scar between their bodies,
stronger, darker, and proud;
how the black cord makes of them a single fabric
that nothing can tear or mend.

JANE HIRSHFIELD

The Price

The fear of loneliness, the wish
to be alone;
love grown rank as seeding grass
in every room,
and anger at it, raging at it,
storming it down.

Also that four-walled chrysalis
and impediment, home;
that lamp and hearth, that easy fit
of bed to bone;
those children, too, sharp witnesses
of all I've done.

My dear, the ropes that bind us
are safe to hold;
the walls that crush us keep us
from the cold.
I know the price and still I pay it, pay it—
words, their furtive kiss,
illicit gold.

ANNE STEVENSON

History

History has many corridors, yes,
and floodlit stages where the folks
with greater parts than we have
romp, cavort, and trade bold gestures
that affect us all,
and sooty alleys where you'd only go
for love or money;
it's a steeply winding stair,
a sliding board, a tunnel or a ramp,
depending on your gravity of mind
or point of view—but all
the same, the level years
like floors that tumble through a burning house
and come to rest, blue cinders,
on the ground where all things subject
to the laws of change must come to rest,
the shelf of now,
this moment over breakfast
as we touch warm fingers over
toast and jam
and say, okay, I'm glad you're here,
no matter what we said or did before,
I'm glad you're here.

JAY PARINI

Air and Fire

From my wife and household and fields
that I have so carefully come to in my time
I enter the craziness of travel,
the reckless elements of air and fire.
Having risen up from my native land,
I find myself smiled at by beautiful women,
making me long for a whole life
to devote to each one, making love to her
in some house, in some way of sleeping
and waking I would make only for her.
And all over the country I find myself
falling in love with houses, woods, and farms
that I will never set foot in.
My eyes go wandering through America,
two wayfaring brothers, resting in silence
against the forbidden gates. O what if
an angel came to me, and said,
"Go free of what you have done. Take
what you want." The atoms of blood
and brain and bone strain apart
at the thought. What I am is the way home.
Like rest after a sleepless night,
my old love comes on me in midair.

                                    WENDELL BERRY

After an Absence

After an absence that was no one's fault
we are shy with each other,
and our words seem younger than we are,
as if we must return to the time we met
and work ourselves back to the present,
the way you never read a story
from the place you stopped
but always start each book all over again.
Perhaps we should have stayed
tied like mountain climbers
by the safe cord of the phone,
its dial our own small prayer wheel,
our voices less ghostly across the miles,
less awkward than they are now.
I had forgotten the grey in your curls,
that splash of winter over your face,
remembering the younger man
you used to be.

And I feel myself turn old and ordinary,
having to think again of food for supper,
the animals to be tended, the whole riptide
of daily life hidden but perilous
pulling both of us under so fast.
I have dreamed of our bed
as if it were a shore where we would be washed up,
not this striped mattress
we must cover with sheets. I had forgotten
all the old business between us,
like mail unanswered so long that silence
becomes eloquent, a message of its own.
I had even forgotten how married love
is a territory more mysterious
the more it is explored, like one of those terrains
you read about, a garden in the desert
where you stoop to drink, never knowing
if your mouth will fill with water or sand.

LINDA PASTAN

from *Asphodel, That Greeny Flower*

All women are not Helen,
                    I know that,
but have Helen in their hearts.
                    My sweet,
                                you have it also, therefore
I love you
                    and could not love you otherwise.
                    Imagine you saw
a field made up of women
                    all silver-white.
                                What should you do
but love them?
                    The storm bursts
                                or fades! it is not
the end of the world.
                    Love is something else,
                                or so I thought it,
a garden which expands,
                    though I knew you as a woman
                                and never thought otherwise,
until the whole sea
                    has been taken up
                                and all its gardens.
It was the love of love,
                    the love that swallows up all else,
                                a grateful love,
a love of nature, of people,
                    animals,
                                a love engendering
gentleness and goodness
                    that moved me
                                and *that* I saw in you.
I should have known
                    though I did not,
                                that the lily-of-the-valley
is a flower makes many ill
                    who whiff it.
                                We had our children,
rivals in the general onslaught.

I put them aside
                though I cared for them
as well as any man
                could care for his children
                        according to my lights.
You understand
                I had to meet you
                        after the event
and have still to meet you.
                Love
                        to which you too shall bow
along with me—
                a flower
                        a weakest flower
shall be our trust
                and not because
                        we are too feeble
to do otherwise
                but because
                        at the height of my power
I risked what I had to do,
                therefore to prove
                        that we love each other
while my very bones sweated
                that I could not cry to you
                        in the act.
Of asphodel, that greeny flower,
                I come, my sweet,
                        to sing to you!

WILLIAM CARLOS WILLIAMS

Love Poem for My Husband

I recognize the need of water—
how a rock, long buried, emerging now,
can bend a river. Last night you cried.
I climbed your back, smoothed your hair
the way I pet the cat, and you
rolled from under me to show your eyes
so that you and I, continents,
could find the seas in all that blue.

Leaves accumulate. I have loved you
half of my life, and still you
build, all day in the woods behind
the house, a stairway to nowhere:
rough-hewn, the redundancy of stones,
thick slugs whose iridescence
only you admire. What draws you
to such silent things?

It is late afternoon. Dusk
informs the blue at the window.
We have been talking
at the kitchen table for hours.
I drift into the landscape
receding from words—
at lunch, you touched my breast
as if I were a girl.

I try to resurrect the mystery
of first love, its coarse grace,
the man whose hands I cannot name.
I have seen you lasso a falling tree,
hold it, bend your breath to root it
in air. You wrestled it gently down,
knuckles raw, vulnerable as the flesh
of a sea turtle, just below the shell.
That's where I want to sting.

BARBARA HELFGOTT HYETT

Twenty-Year Marriage

You keep me waiting in a truck
with its one good wheel stuck in the ditch,
while you piss against the south side of a tree.
Hurry. I've got nothing on under my skirt tonight.
That still excites you, but this pickup has no windows
and the seat, one fake leather thigh,
pressed close to mine is cold.
I'm the same size, shape, make as twenty years ago,
but get inside me, start the engine;
you'll have the strength, the will to move.
I'll pull, you push, we'll tear each other in half.
Come on, baby, lay me down on my back.
Pretend you don't owe me a thing
and maybe we'll roll out of here,
leaving the past stacked up behind us;
old newspapers nobody's ever got to read again.

AI

You must know that I do not love and *that I love you*

You must know that I do not love *and* that I love you,
because everything alive has its two sides;
a word is one wing of the silence,
fire has its cold half.

I love you in order to begin to love you,
to start infinity again
and never to stop loving you:
that's why I do not love you yet.

I love you, and I do not love you, as if I held
keys in my hand: to a future of joy—
a wretched, muddled fate—

My love has two lives, in order to love you:
that's why I love you when I do not love you,
and also why I love you when I do.

PABLO NERUDA
translated by Stephen Tapscott

Our Wives

One rainy night that year we saw our wives
talking together in a barroom mirror.
And as our glasses drained I saw our lives

being lived, and thought how time deceives:
for we had thought of living as the Future,
yet here these lovely women were, our wives,

and we were happy. And yet who believes
that what he's doing now *is* his adventure,
that the beer we're drinking is our lives?

Or think of all the pain that memory leaves,
things we got through we're glad we don't see clearer.
Think of our existence without wives,

our years in England—none of it survives.
It's over, fallen leaves, forgotten weather.
There was a time we thought we'd make our lives

into History. But history thrives
without us: what it leaves us is the future,
a barroom mirror lit up with our wives—
our wives who suddenly became our lives.

JONATHAN GALASSI

Second Marriage

The sense of fifteen years of almost
anything shared is what she sometimes misses
with him, even the awful, silent suppers,
when, with everything already said,
she had longed for words, all over again.
In bed at night, his chest is not
the chest she wept on, learning,
where breast-hair inscribed her cheek,
of onset and ceremony, those whole and open places
that one may fully occupy, like the future.

How happy, even sadly, to have been
young together, to have held off loneliness
with the shiny locket of *we,* as if
whatever could not be found, must, nonetheless,
turn up inside that circle.
Now, neither memory nor need sustains.
She sees the land take shape beneath her,
as birds must, on the first migration,
trusting their bodies as they veer away.
This second love is possible, and chosen.

She wants him. Every broken edge of her
abuts the world, of which he is a portion.

LINDA MCCARRISTON

I Could Take

I could take
two leaves
        and give you one.
Would that not be
a kind of perfection?

But I prefer
one leaf
        torn to give you half
                showing

(after these years, simply)
love's complexity in an act,
        the tearing and
                the unique edges—

one leaf (one word) from the two
imperfections that match.

HAYDEN CARRUTH

For Fran

She packs the flower beds with leaves,
Rags, dampened papers, ties with twine
The lemon tree, but winter carves
Its features on the uprooted stem.

I see the true vein in her neck
And where the smaller ones have broken
Blueing the skin, and where the dark
Cold lines of weariness have eaten

Out through the winding of the bone.
On the hard ground where Adam strayed,
Where nothing but his wants remain,
What do we do to those we need,

To those whose need of us endures
Even the knowledge of what we are?
I turn to her whose future bears
The promise of the appalling air,

My living wife, Frances Levine,
Mother of Theodore, John, and Mark,
Out of whatever we have been
We will make something for the dark.

PHILIP LEVINE

After Paradise

Don't run any more. Quiet. How softly it rains
On the roofs of the city. How perfect
All things are. Now, for the two of you
Waking up in a royal bed by a garret window.
For a man and a woman. For one plant divided
Into masculine and feminine which longed for each other.
Yes, this is my gift to you. Above ashes
On a bitter, bitter earth. Above the subterranean
Echo of clamorings and vows. So that now at dawn
You must be attentive: the tilt of a head,
A hand with a comb, two faces in a mirror
Are only forever once, even if unremembered,
So that you watch what it is, though it fades away,
And are grateful every moment for your being.
Let that little park with greenish marble busts
In the pearl-grey light, under a summer drizzle,
Remain as it was when you opened the gate.
And the street of tall peeling porticos
Which this love of yours suddenly transformed.

CZESLAW MILOSZ

Afternoon Happiness

At a party I spy a handsome psychiatrist,
And wish, as we all do, to get her advice for free.
Doctor, I'll say, I'm supposed to be a poet.
All life's awfulness has been grist to me.
We learn that happiness is a Chinese meal,
While sorrow is a nourishment forever.
My new environment is California Dreamer.
I'm fearful I'm forgetting how to brood.
And, Doctor, another thing has got me worried:
I'm not drinking as much as I should . . .

At home, I want to write a happy poem
On love, or a love poem of happiness.
But they won't do, the tensions of everyday,
The rub, the minor abrasions of any two
Who share one space. Ah, there's no substitute for tragedy!
But in this chapter, tragedy belongs
To that other life, the old life before *us*.
Here is my aphorism of the day:
Happy people are monogamous,
Even in California. So how does the poem play

Without the paraphernalia of betrayal and loss?
I don't have a jealous eye or fear
And neither do you. In truth, I'm fond
Of your ex-mate, whom I name, "my wife-in-law."
My former husband, that old disaster, is now just funny,
So laugh we do, in what Cyril Connolly
Has called the endless, nocturnal conversation
Of marriage. Which may be the best part.
Darling, must I love you in light verse
Without the tribute of profoundest art?

Of course it won't last. You will break my heart
Or I yours, by dying. I could weep over that.
But now it seems forced, here in these heaven hills,
The mourning doves mourning, the squirrels mating,
My old cat warm in my lap, here on our terrace
As from below comes a musical cursing
As you mend my favorite plate. Later of course
I could pick a fight; there is always material in that.
But we don't come from fighting people, those
Who scream out red-hot iambs in their hate.

(break)

No, love, the heavy poem will have to come
From *temps perdu,* fertile with pain, or perhaps
Detonated by terrors far beyond this place
Where the world rends itself, and its tainted waters
Rise in the east to erode our safety here.
Much as I want to gather a lifetime thrift
And craft, my cunning skills tied in a knot for you,
There is only this useless happiness as gift.

CAROLYN KIZER

Marriage Amulet

You are polishing me like old wood.
At night we curl together like two rings
on a dark hand. After many nights,
the rough edges wear down.

If this is aging, it is warm as fleece.
I will gleam like ancient wood.
I will wax smooth, my crags and cowlicks
well-rubbed to show my grain.

Some sage will keep us in his hand for peace.

NANCY WILLARD

Late Loving

> What Christ was saying, what he meant [in the story of Mary
> and Martha] was that the pleasures of that hair, that ointment,
> must be taken. Because the accidents of death would deprive us
> soon enough. We must not deprive ourselves, our loved ones, of
> the luxury of our extravagant affections. We must not try to
> second-guess death by refusing to love the ones we loved . . .
> Mary Gordon, *Final Payments*

If in my mind I marry you every year
it is to calm an extravagance of love
with dousing custom, for it flames up fierce
and wild whenever I forget that we live
in double rooms whose temperature's controlled
by matrimony's turned-down thermostat.
I need the mnemonics, now that we are old,
of oath and law in re-memorizing that.
Our dogs are dead, our child never came true.
I might use up, in my weak-mindedness,
the whole human supply of warmth on you
before I could think of others and digress.
"Love" is finding the familiar dear.
"In Love" is to be taken by surprise.
Over, in the shifty face you wear,
and over, in the assessments of your eyes,
you change, and with new sweet or barbed word
find out new entrances to my inmost nerve.
When you stand at the stove it's I who am most stirred.
When you finish work I rest without reserve.
Daytimes, sometimes, our three-legged race seems slow.
Squabbling onward, we chafe from being so near.
But all night long we lie like crescents of Velcro,
turning together till we re-adhere.
Since you, with longer stride and better vision,
more clearly see the finish line, I stoke
my hurrying self, to keep it in condition,
with light and life-renouncing meals of smoke.
As when a collector scoops two Monarchs in
at once, whose fresh flights to and from each other
are netted down, so in vows I re-imagine
I re-invoke what keeps us stale together.

What you try to give is more than I want to receive,
yet each month when you pick up scissors for our appointment
and my cut hair falls and covers your feet I believe
that the house is filled again with the odor of ointment.

MONA VAN DUYN

from *A Happy Marriage*

Love is the way that lovers never know
Who know the shortest way to find their love,
And never turn aside and never go
By vales beneath nor by the hills above,
But running straight to the familiar door
Break sudden in and call their dear by name
And have their wish and so wish nothing more
And neither know nor trouble how they came.

Love is the path that comes to this same ease
Over the summit of the westward hill,
And feels the rolling of the earth and sees
The sun go down and hears the summer still,
And dips and follows where the orchards fall
And comes here late or never comes at all.

ARCHIBALD MACLEISH

The Old Gray Couple (2)

She: Love, says the poet, has no reasons.

He: Not even after fifty years?

She: Particularly after fifty years.

He: What was it, then, that lured us, that still teases?

She: You used to say my plaited hair!

He: And then you'd laugh.

She: Because it wasn't plaited.
Love had no reasons so you made one up
to laugh at. Look! The old, gray couple!

He: No, to prove the adage true:
Love has no reasons but old lovers do.

She: And they can't tell.

He: I can and so can you.
Fifty years ago we drew each other,
magnetized needle toward the longing north.
It was your naked presence that so moved me.
It was your absolute presence that was love.

She: Ah, *was!*

He: And now, years older, we begin to see
absence not presence: what the world would be
without your footstep in the world—the garden
empty of the radiance where you are.

She: And that's your reason?—that old lovers see
their love because they know now what its loss will be?

He: Because, like Cleopatra in the play,
they know there's nothing left once love's away . . .

She: Nothing remarkable beneath the visiting moon . . .

He: Ours is the late, last wisdom of the afternoon.
We know that love, like light, grows dearer toward the dark.

ARCHIBALD MACLEISH

The Marriage

Incarnate for our marriage you appeared,
Flesh living in the spirit and endeared
By minor graces and slow sensual change.
Through every nerve we made our spirits range.
We fed our minds on every mortal thing:
The lacy fronds of carrots in the spring,
Their flesh sweet on the tongue, the salty wine
From bitter grapes, which gathered through the vine
The mineral drouth of autumn concentrate,
Wild spring in dream escaping, the debate
Of flesh and spirit on those vernal nights,
Its resolution in naive delights,
The young kids bleating softly in the rain—
All this to pass, not to return again.
And when I found your flesh did not resist,
It was the living spirit that I kissed,
It was the spirit's change in which I lay:
Thus, mind in mind we waited for the day.
When flesh shall fall away, and, falling, stand
Wrinkling with shadow over face and hand,
Still I shall meet you on the verge of dust
And know you as a faithful vestige must.
And, in commemoration of our lust,
May our heirs seal us in a single urn,
A single spirit never to return.

YVOR WINTERS

A Marriage

We are made of scenes nights screens pursuits
and flights, corridors and chasms, and I remember
once how you fled into future and, following,

how I caught the train up that coast, sleepless
head on aching arm to a desolate station,
and floated like a shell through those daylong streets,

lost lost and my true love gone into never. Life in a capsule
of fugitive wheels and black and gold of the night coast.
Love lost across water and I alone on the shore.

Did it ever happen? Neither could you endure it,
but entreated me back. Now forty-five years gone,
how many friends rides trains deaths since;

babies grown, rifts lived down and forgotten, houses
outlived: all but the love: we live for
our narrowing future, pass the parlor and wonder

which of us two will have to bury the other.

RICHMOND LATTIMORE

Two Shadows

FOR MADISON

When we are shadows watching over shadows,
when years have passed, enough to live
two lives, when we have passed
through love and come out speechless
on the other side, I will remember
how we spent a night, walking the streets
                              in August, side by side,
following two shadows dressed in long gray coats,
unseasonable clothes they didn't seem to mind,
walking so easily, with easy stride,
merging for a moment, then isolate,
as they led us to your street, your door,
and up the steps until, inside,
love became articulate: eye, lip, and brow.
When we are shadows watching over shadows,
we will not speak of it but *know,* and turn
again toward each other tenderly,
                              shadow to shadow.

ELIZABETH SPIRES

Love Recognized

There are many things in the world and you
Are one of them. Many things keep happening and
You are one of them, and the happening that
Is you keeps falling like snow
On the landscape of not-you, hiding hideousness,
    until
The streets and the world of wrath are choked with
    snow.

How many things have become silent? Traffic
Is throttled. The mayor
Has been, clearly, remiss, and the city
Was totally unprepared for such a crisis. Nor
Was I—yes, why should this happen to me?
I have always been a law-abiding citizen.

But you, like snow, like love, keep falling,

And it is not certain that the world will not be
Covered in a glitter of crystalline whiteness.

Silence.

ROBERT PENN WARREN

To Dorothy

You are not beautiful, exactly.
You are beautiful, inexactly.
You let a weed grow by the mulberry
and a mulberry grow by the house.
So close, in the personal quiet
of a windy night, it brushes the wall
and sweeps away the day till we sleep.

A child said it, and it seemed true:
"Things that are lost are all equal."
But it isn't true. If I lost you,
the air wouldn't move, nor the tree grow.
Someone would pull the weed, my flower.
The quiet wouldn't be yours. If I lost you,
I'd have to ask the grass to let me sleep.

MARVIN BELL

The Widow's Lament in Springtime

Sorrow is my own yard
where the new grass
flames as it has flamed
often before but not
with the cold fire
that closes round me this year.
Thirtyfive years
I lived with my husband.
The plumtree is white today
with masses of flowers.
Masses of flowers
load the cherry branches
and color some bushes
yellow and some red
but the grief in my heart
is stronger than they
for though they were my joy
formerly, today I notice them
and turned away forgetting.
Today my son told me
that in the meadows,
at the edge of the heavy woods
in the distance, he saw
trees of white flowers.
I feel that I would like
to go there
and fall into those flowers
and sink into the marsh near them.

WILLIAM CARLOS WILLIAMS

A Marriage, an Elegy

They lived long, and were faithful
to the good in each other.
They suffered as their faith required.
Now their union is consummate
in earth, and the earth
is their communion. They enter
the serene gravity of the rain,
the hill's passage to the sea.
After long striving, perfect ease.

WENDELL BERRY

XI

Anniversaries: The Progress of Love

The Anniversary

All Kings, and all their favourites,
    All glory of honours, beauties, wits,
The sun itself, which makes times, as they pass,
Is elder by a year now than it was
When thou and I first one another saw:
All other things to their destruction draw,
    Only our love hath no decay;
This no tomorrow hath, nor yesterday,
Running it never runs from us away,
But truly keeps his first, last, everlasting day.

    Two graves must hide thine and my corse;
    If one might, death were no divorce.
Alas, as well as other Princes, we
(Who Prince enough in one another be)
Must leave at last in death these eyes and ears,
Oft fed with true oaths, and with sweet salt tears;
    But souls where nothing dwells but love
(All other thoughts being inmates) then shall prove
This, or a love increasèd there above,
When bodies to their graves, souls from their graves remove.

    And then we shall be throughly blessed;
    But we no more than all the rest.
Here upon earth we're Kings, and none but we
Can be such Kings, nor of such subjects be;
Who is so safe as we? where none can do
Treason to us, except one of us two.
    True and false fears let us refrain,
Let us love nobly, and live, and add again
Years and years unto years, till we attain
To write threescore: this is the second of our reign.

JOHN DONNE

An Anniversary

What we have been becomes
The country where we are.
Spring goes, summer comes,
And in the heat, as one year
Or a thousand years before,
The fields and woods prepare
The burden of their seed
Out of time's wound, the old
Richness of the fall. Their deed
Is renewal. In the household
Of the woods the past
Is always healing in the light,
The high shiftings of the air.
It stands upon its yield
And thrives. Nothing is lost.
What yields, though in despair,
Opens and rises in the night.
Love binds us to this term
With its yes that is crying
In our marrow to confirm
Life that only lives by dying.
Lovers live by the moon
Whose dark and light are one,
Changing without rest.
The root struts from the seed
In the earth's dark—harvest
And feast at the edge of sleep.
Darkened, we are carried
Out of need, deep
In the country we have married.

5/29/72

WENDELL BERRY

from *The Fourteenth Anniversary*

5

then I take my tongue to your body
letting it wander blind over your ribs
as if each were one string of a harp
leaving no string untouched

we reach our hands deep into one another
and if they come up at all
they come up full of poetry the moon
a few stars and a silence rinsed in blood

who dares speak against that silence
let him speak

I have loved you honestly
with all my crooked heart and gently
as darkness comes to water
and in passion with the storm

of all the nothings I have ever said
one word remains
I wear it as a wafer on my tongue
it is your name

6

bind up the sagging breasts of morning
oh my darling let the light in

your hair is more beautiful than dawn

we have arrived years later
at the starting place
now we shall begin again

RICHARD SHELTON

Crystal Anniversary

Deep in a glassy ball, the future looks
Impacted, overdue, a thing that ticks
And dings with promise, but will not happen; we,
Meanwhile, tick-and-dinging through the glow
Of one more married morning, mind the clock
Of age, fading slowly into black-
On-white biographies. The crimson bird
You welcomed sunrise with, and somehow scared,
Has skirred off, blazing, to a hazy past. Still,
It's all there, deep in the glassy ball,
The past as future: you and that morning flash
Of wings bore anniversaries, a rush
Of visions—you, golden on a far-off beach
Sand-silver—anniversary of such
An earlier you, ringed with the flickering churn
Of antique fountains—anniversary again
Of you, you, dazzling in the fever of love
And smiling on those nights we'd hardly move,
But stand for hours, deep in crystal flakes
Of bundled, quiet winter, touching cheeks.
It wasn't then our worst, or yet our best:
It was the first.

PHILIP APPLEMAN

Anniversary

Maybe it wasn't strange to find
drums and cymbals where
there might have been violins, maybe
we couldn't have known; besides,
would it have mattered?
See what the years have left behind:
a thick scar in the palm of my hand,
a ragged one running along the arm.
And you:
I know your scars at midnight
by touch.

Everything we've learned, we've picked up
by ear, a pidgin language
of the heart, just
enough to get by on:
we know the value of cacophony, how to measure
with a broken yardstick,
what to do with bruised fruit.
Reading torn maps, we always
make it home, riding
on empty.

And whatever this is we've built together,
we remember sighting it skew, making it plumb
eventually, and here it stands,
stone over rock. In the walls
there are secret passages
leading to music nobody else can hear,
earthlight nobody else can see. And somewhere
in a room that's not yet finished
there are volumes in our own hand, telling
troubled tales, promises kept, and
promises
still to keep.

PHILIP APPLEMAN

The Underground

There we were in the vaulted tunnel running,
You in your going-away coat speeding ahead
And me, me then like a fleet god gaining
Upon you before you turned to a reed

Or some new white flower japped with crimson
As the coat flapped wild and button after button
Sprang off and fell in a trail
Between the Underground and the Albert Hall.

Honeymooning, moonlighting, late for the Proms,
Our echoes die in that corridor and now
I come as Hansel came on the moonlit stones
Retracing the path back, lifting the buttons

To end up in a draughty lamplit station
After the trains have gone, the wet track
Bared and tensed as I am, all attention
For your step following and damned if I look back.

SEAMUS HEANEY

On the Eve of Our Anniversary

Spring approaches   blowing east
     from Minnesota   still   drifting snow.
Fields   recently black   with birds
     mound   in rows of wind.
Tonight   housebound   you baby
     our plants   spread paper
dump pots   exposing   the married roots.
     Purple shade   of the passion leaf.
Pale stems   of coleus.
     Strands   of spider shoots.
The dog stretches   beside you   noses
     into the damp dirt   sniffing for something
like herself.   She finds   your hand
     You hold   a baby tears.
I admire each heart   each head-shaped leaf
     even   its miniature   milkweed flower
barely   there   a fairy hand   you insist I see
     and touch.   Dear   this March   as snow
comes and goes   as we pair   wedding ourselves
     again   pray   these roots too   outgrow their pots
yet growing   still   the wind will keep us in
     to trim   and feed
this spring   these plants   our rings.

GARY MARGOLIS

An Anniversary: A Lucubration

I.

Marriage isn't, after all, a prison;
Nor a chancery court where every decision
Goes against both the defendant and plaintiff;
Nor a plaintive
Duet in an old-fashioned birdcage whose cover
Is replaced by the owner when day is over;
Nor a long lease on a bridal suite,
Every stitch prinked in yellowing white:
The infinity of hell
In a small hotel;
Nor, unlike courtship, a paper chase
After a face
That turns out to be foolscap in the end
And goes to ground;
Nor a delighted pairing
Of the attributes we were wearing
When love struck, a gestalt
Consonant to a fault;
Nor a silent contract
Of service in the abstract,
Printed, patient, in the concrete
Earth beneath our feet;
Not a universal journey in the dark;
Not a short walk in the park;
Not a kind of unheard singing;
Not a conditioning bell ringing;
Not an exaltation;
Not a condonation;
Not, in fact, a thing
Like loving.

II.

Marriage, after all, is ordinary,
Like looking at a prairie.
The best of it
Is you get used to it.
After untold episodes of hope
And giving pearly fancies too much rope
And falling in between into despair

And finally arriving there—
The run-down, shut-up station with a lone
Baggage cart under an arc lamp and no one
To meet you and no town and your lit train
Pulling away west in the rain—
You finally realize you've arrived
At all there is to having lived.
And that's when anything that's going to happen does:
The first humane exchange of selfish lies,
The first unprogrammed anger,
The first perception that a stranger
Inhabits your present and will inherit
Your future, irrespective of her merit;
The first dispassionate
Appraisal of her person for the cash in it;
The first unexpected Doppler
Effect—like the rattle of a poplar
Hushed suddenly—of the silver of her laughter
Here now and real and still here after
It has died away;
The first real earthbound day
You two trudge out in unison
Under the pendulous arc lamp of the sun
To find your station,
However humble, in a failing nation
Where one from many has no valid voice
These days, and one from two must make a choice
To keep themselves by being ordinary;
By looking, while the light lasts, at the prairie.

L. E. SISSMAN

Our Twentieth Wedding Anniversary

(ELIZABETH)

Leaves espaliered jade on our barn's loft window,
sky stretched on a two-pane sash . . . it doesn't open:
stab of roofdrip, this leaf, that leaf twings,
an assault the heartless leaf rejects.
The picture is too perfect for our lives:
in Chardin's stills, the paint bleeds, juice is moving.
We have weathered the wet of twenty years.
Many cripples have won their place in the race;
Immanuel Kant remained unmarried and sane,
no one could Byronize his walk to class.
Often the player outdistances the game. . . .
This week is our first this summer to go unfretted;
we smell as green as the weeds that bruise the flower—
a house eats up the wood that made it.

ROBERT LOWELL

Anniversary on the Island

The long waves glide in through the afternoon
while we watch from the island
from the cool shadow under the trees where the long ridge
a fold in the skirt of the mountain
runs down to the end of the headland

day after day we wake to the island
the light rises through the drops on the leaves
and we remember like birds where we are
night after night we touch the dark island
that once we set out for

and lie still at last with the island in our arms
hearing the leaves and the breathing shore
there are no years any more
only the one mountain
and on all sides the sea that brought us

W. S. MERWIN

Lines on a Tenth Anniversary

What she's wearing is the brightest thing in the kitchen,
And that's not much. She's ironing, the iron

Puffing out its own white clouds above a skirt.
I've stopped reading about the broken parts

Of men in the wet assembly lines
And the man with a carnation at his throat

Who wants to sell us the necessities of life.
It is good, I think,

To be sitting in a warm room
While the lawn whitens with frost.

It is good, too,
Still to be in love,

Or whatever
That tune has come to through the years.

ARTHUR SMITH

Celebration for June 24

FOR MARIAN

Before you, I was living on an island
And all around the seas of that lonely coast
Cast up their imitation jewels, cast
Their fables and enigmas, questioning, sly.
I never solved them, or ever even heard,
Being perfect in innocence, unconscious of self;
Such ignorance of history was all my wealth—
A geographer sleeping in the shadow of virgins.

But though my maps were made of private countries
I was a foreigner in all of them after you had come,
For when you spoke, it was with a human tongue
And never understood by my land-locked gentry.
Then did the sun shake down a million bells
And birds bloom on bough in wildest song!
Phlegmatic hills went shivering with flame;
The chestnut trees were manic at their deepest boles!

It is little strange that nature was riven in her frame
At this second creation, known to every lover—
How we are shaped and shape ourselves in the desires of the other
Within the tolerance of human change.
Out of the spring's innocence this revolution,
Created on a kiss, announced the second season,
The summer of private history, of growth, through whose sweet
     sessions
The trees lift toward the sun, each leaf a revelation.

Our bodies, coupled in the moonlight's album
Proclaimed our love against the outlaw times
Whose signature was written in the burning towns.
Your face against the night was my medallion.
Your coming forth aroused unlikely trumpets
In the once-tame heart. They heralded your worth
Who are my lodestar, my bright and ultimate North,
Marrying all points of my personal compass.

(break)

This is the love that now invents my fear
Which nuzzles me like a puppy each violent day.
It is poor comfort that the mind comes, saying:
What is one slim girl to the peoples' wars?
Still, my dice are loaded: having had such luck,
Having your love, my life would still be whole
Though I should die tomorrow. I have lived it all.
—And love is never love, that cannot give love up.

Thomas McGrath

The Progress of Love

from Three Anniversaries

It's been ten years since first your body
Fell out of the sky into my hands.
You were for me such a simple rain
And I caught you so thoughtlessly. Love,
Then all the colors of our touching
Were primary, and green was our bed.

The weather that came into that bed
Wildly spun the vane of the body
And blew us through landscapes of touching.
It was rich soil we held in our hands,
Though we thought merely to dream of love
Would make it leaf out, rain or no rain.

Such dreaming brought us a storm of rain.
We stood in it and stood it. The bed
We slept in held the shape of our love
Rough hewn by inclemency. Body
To body, we studied with our hands
The ways of gentling wind by touching,

The wind that mixed the colors. Touching
Each other, we learned to make a rain
That washed clean the world between our hands,
Though all the while something shook our bed.
On the trembling ground of the body,
We surveyed to build a house of love.

Such innocence! We didn't know love
Turns into snow. O, it was touching,
What we didn't know. So your body
Taught my body and mine yours how rain,
Transformed all beautifully, fills bed
After bed with toys for empty hands.

And when we began to spread our hands
Skyward and wait for the falling love,
Our own sea-change took place in that bed:
We saw how a cold shadow touching
All things deepened them beyond mere rain;
We marked the seasons of the body.

(break)

Now there's nothing our hands aren't touching:
We've come to love what happens to rain.
I turn in bed and graze your body.

PHILIP DACEY

25th Anniversary

There is something I want
to tell you beyond love
or gratitude or sex, beyond
irritation or a purer anger.
For years I have hoarded
your small faults the way
I might hoard kindling
towards some future conflagration,
and from the moment you broke
into my life, all out of breath,
I have half expected you
to break back out.
But here we are
like the married couple
from Cerveteri who smile
from their 6th-century sarcophagus
as if they are giving a party.
How young we were in Rome, buying
their portraits on postcards,
thinking that we too
were entangled already
beyond amputation, beyond
even death, as we are
as we are now.

LINDA PASTAN

Three Poems for a Twenty-fifth Anniversary

1. Housecleaning

after returning
all the tools I borrowed
from neighbors and friends
and the books to the library

I am amazed to find
so many things around the house
like you
that really belong here

I had thought
you were on loan and overdue
the fines were mounting into millions
I could never pay them

so for twenty-five years
I looked everyone straight in the eyes
pretending you were mine
and I kept you

2. Building

you built your house
on my wavering sands

I built my house on yours
and we abide

you are afraid of water
I am afraid of winds

you hold me during hurricanes
I keep you from the tide

3. Grandfathering

it is time for grandfathering
and I don't know how
leave me alone I have served my turn
I will run away

(break)

then I see your hand
after so many years still pale
and slender as a wand
reach out to touch a child

and I hear you say
when it was time for fathering
you found the way
as you will now

RICHARD SHELTON

The Commemoration

I wish I could proclaim
My faith enshrined in you
And spread among a few
Our high but hidden fame,
That we new life have spun
Past all that's thought and done,
And someone or no one
Might tell both did the same.

Material things will pass
And we have seen the flower
And the slow falling tower
Lie gently in the grass,
But meantime we have stored
Riches past bed and board
And nursed another hoard
Than callow lad and lass.

Invisible virtue now
Expands upon the air
Although no fruit appear
Nor weight bend down the bough,
And harvests truly grown
For someone or no one
Are stored and safely won
In hollow heart and brow.

How can one thing remain
Except the invisible,
The echo of a bell
Long rusted in the rain?
This strand we weave into
Our monologue of two,
And time cannot undo
That strong and subtle chain.

EDWIN MUIR

To My Wife
on Our Thirty-fifth Wedding Anniversary

from Songs of a Wanderer

Enmeshed in the frenzies of praying mantises.
Of Nature's creations, what is more sublime
than a family? Wife, husband, child—
the golden division of the species, the lesser becomes the greater,
and so the tribe renews itself in the festoons of time.
    O, mountain stream
    Basalt beneath
    Bedrock of flight
    Pendulum-home
    Vise of the heart
    Lily of the soul
    Contralto of quiet
    And faithful shroud.
    Violet—sorrow,
    In winter flakes,
    O, you warm earth
    Of peaks and valleys!
    In sickness and in health
    Siamese sister
    My Bride.

ALEKSANDER WAT
translated by Czeslaw Milosz and Leonard Nathan

Anniversary Sonnet

Stopping to rest, we washed our hands
in the river, do you remember?
What are those dark fish, you asked.
What happens to them will happen to us.

I thought, It is simple to be a man,
simple to be a woman if we love
what is brief, what is given to us,
and clear the gloom with it.

We stood up, walked back to the world.
The sunset deepened the house's hush.
What marvelous lives we live, you said,
without saying anything at all.

Our children, sunlight on the wall.
On our tongues, the past, a drop of gold.

MAURYA SIMON

Acknowledgments

Grateful acknowledgment is made to the publishers or publications from which the poems in this volume were reprinted. Unless specifically noted otherwise, copyright of the poems is held by the individual poets.

DANNIE ABSE: "Epithalamion" from *White Coat, Purple Coat (Collected Poems 1948–88)* by Dannie Abse. Copyright © 1977, 1989 by Dannie Abse. Reprinted by permission of the Anthony Sheil Agency on behalf of the author.

AI: "Twenty-Year Marriage" from *Cruelty* by Ai. Copyright © 1970, 1973 by Ai. Reprinted by permission of Houghton Mifflin Company.

YEHUDA AMICHAI: "Advice for good love" by Yehuda Amichai from *Selected Poetry of Yehuda Amichai,* translated by Chana Block. Copyright © 1986 by Chana Block and Stephen Mitchell. Reprinted by permission of Harper & Row, Publishers, Inc.

PHILIP APPLEMAN: "Ars Poetica" from *Open Doorways* (W. W. Norton & Company, 1976); "Anniversary" from *Let There Be Light* (HarperCollins, 1991); "Crystal Anniversary" from *Summer Love and Surf* (Vanderbilt University Press, 1968) by Philip Appleman. Reprinted by permission of the author.

MARGARET ATWOOD: "Habitation" from Margaret Atwood's *Selected Poems, 1966–1984.* Copyright © Margaret Atwood, 1990; reprinted by permission of Oxford University Press Canada.

ROBIN BECKER: "A Marriage" reprinted from *Giacometti's Dog* by Robin Becker, by permission of the University of Pittsburgh Press. Copyright © 1990 by Robin Becker.

MARVIN BELL: "To Dorothy" from *Stars Which See, Stars Which Do Not See* (Atheneum, 1977); *New and Selected Poems* (Atheneum, 1987) by Marvin Bell. Copyright © 1977 by Marvin Bell. Reprinted by permission of the author.

GREGORY CORSO: "Marriage" from *The Happy Birthday of Death* by Gregory Corso. Copyright © 1960 by New Directions Publishing Corporation. Reprinted by permission of New Directions Publishing Corporation.

ROBERT CREELEY: "For Love" from *Collected Poems of Robert Creeley, 1945–1975,* copyright © 1983 The Regents of the University of California. Used by Permission.

PHILIP DACEY: "Three Anniversaries," Section 2, "The Progress of Love" from *The Boy Under the Bed* by Philip Dacey, The Johns Hopkins University Press, Baltimore/London, 1981, pp. 64–65. Used by Permission.

PETER DAVISON: "Equinox 1980" from *The Great Ledge* by Peter Davison. Copyright © 1989 by Peter Davison. Reprinted by permission of Alfred A. Knopf, Inc.

GREG DELANTY: "Thrust & Parry" is reprinted by permission of the author.

BABETTE DEUTSCH: "They Came to the Wedding" from *The Collected Poems of Babette Deutsch* (Doubleday & Company, 1969) by Babette Deutsch. Reprinted by permission of the author.

ALAN DUGAN: "Love Song: I and Thou," copyright © 1961, 1962, 1968, 1972, 1973, 1974, 1983 by Alan Dugan. From *New and Collected Poems, 1961–1983,* first published by the Ecco Press in 1983. Reprinted by Permission.

DOUGLAS DUNN: "From the Night-Window" is reprinted from *Terry Street* (Faber and Faber Ltd., 1971) by Douglas Dunn. Used by Permission.

STEPHEN DUNN: "The Night the Children Were Away," "After the Argument," and "Letter Home" from *Local Time* by Stephen Dunn. Copyright © 1986 by the author. Reprinted by permission of William Morrow & Co. "Epithalamion" is reprinted from *Landscape at the End of the Century* by Stephen Dunn, by permission of W. W. Norton & Company, Inc. Copyright © 1991 by Stephen Dunn.

PAUL DURCAN: "At the Funeral of the Marriage" and "Hymn to a Broken Marriage" by Paul Durcan are reprinted by permission of The Black Staff Press on behalf of the author.

ALAN FELDMAN: "Omens" and "A Man and a Woman" from *The Happy Genius* (SUN, 1978) by Alan Feldman. Copyright © 1978 by Alan Feldman. Reprinted by permission of the author.

Donald Finkel: "Marriage" from *Selected Shorter Poems* (Atheneum, 1987) by Donald Finkel. Copyright © 1964 by Donald Finkel. Reprinted by permission of the author.

Charles Fishman: "Patience" appeared originally in *Redstart.* "Patience" and "The Message" are reprinted by permission of the author.

Jonathan Galassi: "Our Wives" from *Morning Run* (British American Publishing, 1988) by Jonathan Galassi. Copyright © 1988 by Jonathan Galassi. Reprinted by permission of the author.

Amy Gerstler: "Marriage" is excerpted from *Bitter Angel,* copyright © 1989 by Amy Gerstler. Published by North Point Press and reprinted by permission.

Dana Gioia: "The Country Wife" from *Daily Horoscope* by Dana Gioia. Copyright © 1986 by Dana Gioia. Reprinted by permission of Graywolf Press.

Louise Glück: "Horse," copyright © 1985 by Louise Glück. From *The Triumph of Achilles,* first published by the Ecco Press in 1985. Reprinted by Permission. "Here Are My Black Clothes," copyright © 1971, 1972, 1973, 1974, 1975 by Louise Glück. From *The House on Marshland,* first published by the Ecco Press in 1975. Reprinted by Permission.

Patricia Goedicke: "The Husband and Wife Team" from *The Wind of Our Going* (Copper Canyon Press, 1985) by Patricia Goedicke. Reprinted by permission of Copper Canyon Press.

Robert Graves: "A Slice of Wedding Cake" and "The Wedding" from *Collected Poems,* copyright © 1975 by Robert Graves. Reprinted by permission of A. P. Watt Limited on behalf of The Trustees of the Robert Graves Copyright Trust.

Linda Gregg: "Trouble in the Portable Marriage" and "No More Marriages" from *Too Bright to See* by Linda Gregg. Copyright © 1981 by Linda Gregg. Reprinted by permission of Graywolf Press.

Rachel Hadas: "That Walk Away as One: A Marriage Brood," Section 10, copyright © 1987 by Rachel Hadas. Reprinted from *A Son from Sleep* by permission of University Press of New England.

Donald Hall: Excerpt from "To Build a House" from *The One Day* by Donald Hall. Copyright © 1988 by Donald Hall. Reprinted by permission of Ticknor & Fields, a Houghton Mifflin Company.

DANIEL HALPERN: "Epithalamium" from *Tango* by Daniel Halpern. Copyright © 1987 by Daniel Halpern. Used by permission of Viking Penguin, a division of Penguin Books USA Inc.

MICHAEL HAMBURGER: "Mathematics of Love" from *Michael Hamburger: Collected Poems* (Carcanet Press, 1985) by Michael Hamburger. Reprinted by permission of the author.

SEAMUS HEANEY: "A Pillowed Head" copyright © 1990 by Seamus Heaney. Reprinted by permission of the author. "Wedding Day" and "Poem" from *Poems, 1965–1975* by Seamus Heaney. Copyright © 1966, 1969, 1972, 1975, 1980 by Seamus Heaney. Reprinted by permission of Farrar, Straus & Giroux, Inc. "The Skunk" from *Selected Poems, Nineteen Sixty-Nine to Nineteen Eighty-Seven* by Seamus Heaney, copyright © 1990 by Seamus Heaney. Reprinted by permission of Farrar, Straus & Giroux. "The Underground" from *Station Island* by Seamus Heaney. Copyright © 1985 by Seamus Heaney. Reprinted by permission of Farrar, Straus & Giroux, Inc.

BARBARA HELFGOTT HYETT: "Love Poem for My Husband" from *Natural Law* (Northland Press of Winona, 1989) by Barbara Helfgott Hyett. Copyright © 1989 by Barbara Helfgott Hyett. Reprinted by permission of the author.

JANE HIRSCHFIELD: "For What Binds Us" copyright © 1988 by Jane Hirschfield. Reprinted from *Gravity and Angels* by permission of University Press of New England.

DAVID IGNATOW: "Marriage," copyright © 1970 by David Ignatow. Reprinted from *Poems, 1934–1969*, Wesleyan University Press by permission of University Press of New England.

RANDALL JARRELL: Excerpt from the poem "Woman" copyright © 1963 by Randall Jarrell. Reprinted by permission of the Rhoda Weyr Agency.

DONALD JUSTICE: "But That Is Another Story" from *Selected Poems* (Atheneum, 1979) by Donald Justice. Copyright © 1979 by Donald Justice. Reprinted by permission of the author.

PETER KAROFF: "Ways of Looking at a Wife" and "Two-Part Harmony" from an unpublished manuscript currently titled *Domestic Issues*. Reprinted by permission of the author.

GALWAY KINNELL: "After Making Love We Hear Footsteps" from *Mortal Acts, Mortal Words* by Galway Kinnell. Copyright © 1980 by Galway Kinnell. Reprinted by permission of Houghton Mifflin Company.

SUSAN KINSOLVING: "A Bride Again" is reprinted by permission of the author.

CAROLYN KIZER: "Afternoon Happiness" from *YIN: New Poems* (Boa Editions, 1984) by Carolyn Kizer, which received the Pulitzer Prize in 1985. Reprinted by permission of the author.

MAXINE KUMIN: "Homecoming" from *Up Country* (Harper & Row, 1972) by Maxine Kumin. Reprinted by permission of Curtis Brown, Ltd. Copyright © 1961 by Maxine Kumin. First published in *The New Yorker*.

STANLEY KUNITZ: "River Road" reprinted from *The Testing-Tree* by Stanley Kunitz. Copyright © 1966 by Stanley Kunitz. "Foreign Affairs" is reprinted from *Selected Poems, 1928–1958* by Stanley Kunitz. Copyright © 1958 by Stanley Kunitz. Used by permission of Little, Brown and Company.

PHILIP LARKIN: "To My Wife" from *Collected Poems* by Philip Larkin. Copyright © 1988, 1989 by the Estate of Philip Larkin. Reprinted by permission of Farrar, Straus & Giroux, Inc. "Wedding-Wind" from *The Less Deceived* by Philip Larkin. Reprinted by permission of The Marvell Press, England.

RICHMOND LATTIMORE: "A Marriage" reprinted by permission of Louisiana State University Press from *Continuing Conclusions* by Richard Lattimore. Copyright © 1983 by Richmond Lattimore.

DENISE LEVERTOV: "The Wife" from *Collected Earlier Poems 1940–1960*. Copyright © 1959 by Denise Levertov Goodman. "The Ache of Marriage" and "Wedding Ring" from *Poems, 1960–1967*. Copyright © 1964 by Denise Levertov Goodman. Reprinted by permission of New Directions Publishing Corporation.

PHILIP LEVINE: "For Fran" from *On the Edge* (The Stone Wall Press, 1963) by Philip Levine. Copyright © Philip Levine. Reprinted by permission of the author.

ROBERT LOWELL: "Man and Wife" and "Our Twentieth Wedding Anniversary" from *Selected Poems* by Robert Lowell. Copyright © 1958, 1973, 1976 by Robert Lowell. Renewal copyright © 1986 by the Estate of Robert Lowell. Reprinted by permission of Farrar, Straus & Giroux, Inc.

ARCHIBALD MACLEISH: "A Happy Marriage" and "The Old Gray Couple (2)" from *New and Collected Poems: 1917–1982* by Archibald MacLeish. Copyright © 1985 by the Estate of

Archibald MacLeish. Reprinted by permission of Houghton Mifflin Company.

GARY MARGOLIS: "Some Nation Who's Been Slighted" appeared originally in *Poetry* magazine. "On the Eve of Our Anniversary" from *The Day We Still Stand Here* (University of Georgia Press, 1983) by Gary Margolis. Reprinted by permission of the author.

GAIL MAZUR: "Leaving" is reprinted by permission of the author.

LINDA McCARRISTON: "Second Marriage" from *Talking Soft Dutch* (Texas Tech University Press, 1984) by Linda McCarriston. Reprinted by permission of the author.

THOMAS McGRATH: "Celebration for June 24" from *Selected Poems of Thomas McGrath, 1938–88* (Copper Canyon Press, 1988) by Thomas McGrath. Reprinted by permission of Copper Canyon Press.

HEATHER McHUGH: "Domestic Song" from *Dangers* by Heather McHugh. Copyright © 1977 by Heather McHugh. Reprinted by permission of Houghton Mifflin Company.

SANDRA McPHERSON: "7, 22, 66," copyright © 1979, 1980, 1981, 1982 by Sandra McPherson. From *Patron Happiness,* first published by The Ecco Press in 1983. Reprinted by Permission.

WILLIAM MEREDITH: "Tree Marriage" from *Partial Accounts* by William Meredith. Copyright © 1987 by William Meredith. Reprinted by permission of Alfred A. Knopf, Inc.

JAMES MERRILL: "Upon a Second Marriage" appeared originally in *Divine Comedies* (Atheneum, 1976) by James Merrill. Copyright © 1982 by James Merrill. Reprinted by permission of the author.

W. S. MERWIN: "Anniversary on the Island" from *The Rain in the Trees* by W. S. Merwin. Copyright © 1988 by W. S. Merwin. Reprinted by permission of Alfred A. Knopf, Inc.

EDNA ST. VINCENT MILLAY: "Oh, Think Not I Am Faithful to a Vow!" by Edna St. Vincent Millay. From *Collected Sonnets,* Revised and Expanded Edition, Harper & Row, 1988. Copyright © 1922, 1950 by Edna St. Vincent Millay. Reprinted by permission of Elizabeth Barnett, Literary Executor.

VASSAR MILLER: "Song for a Marriage," reprinted from *Wage War on Silence* by Vassar Miller © 1960 by Vassar Miller, Wesleyan University Press, by permission of University Press of New England.

CZESLAW MILOSZ: "After Paradise," copyright © 1988 by Czeslaw Milosz Royalties, Inc. From *The Collected Poems, 1931–1987*, first published by The Ecco Press in 1988. Reprinted by Permission.

LISEL MUELLER: "The Blind Leading the Blind" from *Learning to Play by Ear* by Lisel Mueller. Copyright © 1990 by Lisel Mueller. Reprinted by permission of Juniper Press.

EDWIN MUIR: "The Commemoration" from *Collected Poems* by Edwin Muir. Copyright © 1969 by Willa Muir. Reprinted by permission of Oxford University Press.

PAUL MULDOON: "Identities" from *Selected Poems, 1968–86*, copyright © 1973, 1977, 1980, 1983, 1986, 1987 by Paul Muldoon. Published in 1987 by The Ecco Press. Reprinted by Permission.

HOWARD NEMEROV: "The Common Wisdom" from *The Collected Poems of Howard Nemerov* (University of Chicago Press, 1977) by Howard Nemerov. "Adam and Eve in Later Life" from *Inside the Onion* (University of Chicago Press, 1984) by Howard Nemerov. Reprinted by permission of the author.

PABLO NERUDA: "You must know that I do not love *and* that I love you" and "Love crosses its islands, from grief to grief" are reprinted from *100 Love Sonnets* by Pablo Neruda, translated by Stephen Tapscott, copyright © Pablo Neruda, 1959, copyright © 1986, University of Texas Press. By permission of the University of Texas Press.

NAOMI SHIHAB NYE: "So Much Happiness" from *Hugging the Jukebox* (E. P. Dutton, 1982, Breitenbush Books, 1986) by Naomi Shihab Nye. Reprinted by permission of the author.

SHARON OLDS: "Primitive" is reprinted from *Satan Says,* by Sharon Olds, by permission of the University of Pittsburgh Press. Copyright © 1980 by Sharon Olds. Used by Permission. "Poem to My Husband from My Father's Daughter" from *The Dead and the Living* by Sharon Olds. Copyright © 1983 by Sharon Olds. Reprinted by permission of Alfred A. Knopf, Inc.

JOEL OPPENHEIMER: "A Prayer" reprinted with permission of Macmillan Publishing Company from *On Occasion* by Joel Oppenheimer. Copyright © 1974 by Joel Oppenheimer.

STEVE ORLEN: "Love and Memory" from *A Place at the Table* (Holt, Rinehart and Winston, 1981) by Steve Orlen. Reprinted by permission of the author.

ALICIA OSTRIKER: "The Marriage Nocturne" reprinted from *The Imaginary Lover* by Alicia Ostriker, by permission of the University of Pittsburgh Press. Copyright © 1986 by Alicia Ostriker.

ROBERT PACK: "You Hold Me in My Life" from *Home from the Cemetery* by Robert Pack. Copyright © 1969 by Rutgers, the State University of New Jersey. Reprinted by permission of Rutgers University Press.

THERESA PAPPAS: "Possession" appeared originally in *North Dakota Quarterly*, 57, No. 3 (1989). Reprinted by permission of the author.

JAY PARINI: "History" from *Town Life: Poems* by Jay Parini. Copyright © 1988 by Jay Parini. Reprinted by permission of Henry Holt and Company, Inc.

LINDA PASTAN: "25th Anniversary," "Drift," "Ark," and "Because" are reprinted from *PM/AM, New and Selected Poems,* by Linda Pastan, by permission of W. W. Norton & Company, Inc. Copyright © 1982 by Linda Pastan. "After an Absence" is reprinted from *The Imperfect Paradise, Poems* by Linda Pastan, by permission of W. W. Norton & Company, Inc. Copyright © 1988 by Linda Pastan.

MARGE PIERCY: "Witnessing a Wedding" from *My Mother's Body* by Marge Piercy. Copyright © 1985 by Marge Piercy. Reprinted by permission of Alfred A. Knopf, Inc.

CHRISTINE DE PISAN: "In Praise of Marriage" is reprinted from *Ballads, Rondeaux, Virelais: An Anthology,* Leicester University Press, 1965. Used by Permission.

SYLVIA PLATH: "Wreath for a Bridal" from *The Collected Poems of Sylvia Plath,* edited by Ted Hughes. Copyright © 1960, 1965, 1971, 1981 by the Estate of Sylvia Plath. Reprinted by permission of Harper & Row, Publisher, Inc.

JOHN CROWE RANSOM: "Winter Remembered" from *Selected Poems,* copyright © 1924, 1927, 1934, 1939, 1945, 1962, 1963, 1969 by Alfred A. Knopf, Inc. Copyright renewed 1952, 1954 by John Crowe Ransom. Issued in 1978 by The Ecco Press and reprinted by permission.

DAVID RAY: "Marriage" from *The Touched Life* (Scarecrow Press, 1982) by David Ray. First appeared in *The Tramps Cup* (The Chariton Review Press, 1978). Reprinted by permission of the author.

ALASTAIR REID: "Outlook Uncertain" and "The Figures on the Frieze" from *Weathering: Poems and Translations* (University of Georgia Press, 1988) by Alastair Reid. Reprinted by permission of the author.

SAPPHO: "O Bride" is reprinted from *Sappho: A New Translation* by Mary Barnard. Copyright © 1958 The Regents of the University of California; © renewed 1984 by Mary Barnard. Used by permission.

GRACE SCHULMAN: "After the Division" appeared originally in *Poetry* magazine. Reprinted by permission of the author.

DELMORE SCHWARTZ: "Will you perhaps consent to be" from *Selected Poems: Summer Knowledge.* Copyright © 1958, 1959 by Delmore Schwartz. Reprinted by permission of New Directions Publishing Corporation.

ANNE SEXTON: "Divorce" from *45 Mercy Street* by Anne Sexton. Copyright © 1976 by Linda Gray Sexton and Loring Conant, Jr. Reprinted by permission of Houghton Mifflin Company.

RICHARD SHELTON: Excerpt from "The Fourteenth Anniversary," Parts 5 and 6, and "Three Poems for a Twenty-fifth Anniversary" are reprinted from *Selected Poems, 1969–1981,* by Richard Shelton, by permission of the University of Pittsburgh Press. Copyright © 1982 by Richard Shelton.

MAURYA SIMON: "Anniversary Sonnet" from *Days of Awe* (Copper Canyon Press, 1989) by Maurya Simon. Reprinted by permission of Copper Canyon Press.

L. E. SISSMAN: "Man and Wife" and "An Anniversary: A Lucubration" are reprinted from *Hello Darkness: The Collected Poems of L. E. Sissman* by L. E. Sissman. Copyright © 1963, 1964, 1965, 1966, 1967, 1968, 1969, 1970, 1971 by L. E. Sissman. Copyright © 1971, 1973, 1974, 1976, 1977, 1978 by Anne B. Sissman. Used by permission of Little, Brown and Company.

ARTHUR SMITH: "Good-bye. Sweet Dreams. Come Back." and "Lines on a Tenth Anniversary" are reprinted from *Elegy on Independence Day* by Arthur Smith, by permission of the University of Pittsburgh Press. Copyright © 1985 by Arthur Smith.

DAVE SMITH: "Just Married" from *The Roundhouse Voices* by Dave Smith. Copyright © 1985 by Dave Smith. Reprinted by permission of Harper & Row, Publishers, Inc.

W. D. Snodgrass: "A Locked House" from *Selected Poems, 1957–1987.* Copyright © 1983, 1986, by W. D. Snodgrass. Reprinted by permission of Soho Press, Inc.

Marcia Southwick: "The Wedding" from *The Night Won't Save Anyone* by Marcia Southwick. Copyright © 1980 by the University of Georgia Press. Used by Permission.

Elizabeth Spires: "Two Shadows" from *Swan's Island* (Henry Holt, 1985) by Elizabeth Spires. Copyright © 1985 by Elizabeth Spires. Reprinted by permission of the author.

Wallace Stevens: "Notes toward a Supreme Fiction" (Part 4). Copyright © 1942 by Wallace Stevens. Reprinted from *The Collected Poems of Wallace Stevens* by permission of Alfred A. Knopf, Inc.

Anne Stevenson: "The Price" copyright © Anne Stevenson, 1987. Reprinted from Anne Stevenson's *Selected Poems, 1956–1986* (1987) by permission of Oxford University Press.

Mark Strand: "The Marriage" reprinted with permission of Atheneum Publishers, an imprint of Macmillan Publishing Company, from *Reasons for Moving* by Mark Strand. Copyright © 1968 by Mark Strand.

Mark Van Doren: "Marriage" from *Collected and New Poems* by Mark Van Doren. Copyright © 1963 by Mark Van Doren. Reprinted by permission of Hill and Wang, a division of Farrar, Straus & Giroux, Inc.

Mona Van Duyn: "Toward a Definition of Marriage," Section 5, reprinted with permission of Atheneum Publishers, an imprint of Macmillan Publishing Company, from *Merciful Disguises* by Mona Van Duyn. Copyright © 1959, 1973 by Mona Van Duyn. "Late Loving" from *Near Changes* by Mona Van Duyn. Copyright © 1990 by Mona Van Duyn. Reprinted by permission of Alfred A. Knopf, Inc.

Ellen Bryant Voight: "A Marriage Poem," "For My Husband," "Liebesgedicht," and "Quarrel" reprinted from *The Forces of Plenty* by Ellen Bryant Voight, by permission of W. W. Norton & Company, Inc. Copyright © 1983 by Ellen Bryant Voight. "The Marriage," copyright © 1976 by Ellen Voight. Reprinted from *Claiming Kin* by permission of the University Press of New England.

Robert Penn Warren: "Love Recognized" from *Now and Then: Poems, 1976–1987* by Robert Penn Warren. Copyright